ASS ISAIAH 40:6

THE IRISH BEEF BOOK

The
Irish Beef
Book

Pat Whelan
and Katy McGuinness

Gill Books

GILL BOOKS
HUME AVENUE
PARK WEST
DUBLIN 12
www.gillbooks.ie

Gill Books is an imprint of M.H. Gill & Co.

© Pat Whelan and Katy McGuinness 2013

978 0717 5594 1

DESIGN BY www.grahamthew.com
FOOD COOKED BY Katy McGuinness and Rebecca Rowe
PHOTOGRAPHY © Joanne Murphy
PHOTOS ON pp. 81, 96, 182-83 © Moya McAllister
ILLUSTRATION on p. 21 © Classic Image/Alamy
PHOTOGRAPHER'S ASSISTANT: Liosa Mac Namara
STYLISTS: Carly Horan and Blondie Horan
PROPS KINDLY SUPPLIED BY: Ashley Cottage Interiors, Tralee, Co. Kerry; Avoca, Avoca Kilmacanogue, Bray, Co. Wicklow, Tel: +353 1
274 6939, www.avoca.ie; Marks & Spencer, Dundrum Town Centre, Tel: (01) 299 1300, www.marksandspencer.ie; Meadows & Byrne,
Dún Laoghaire, Co. Dublin, Tel: (01)280 4554; Historic Interiors, Oberstown, Lusk, Co. Dublin, Tel: (01) 843 7174, Email: killian@
historicinteriors.net; Two Wooden Horses,
Chapel Road, Greystones, Wicklow, Tel: (083) 405 6492
INDEXED BY Adam Pozner
PRINTED BY Printer Trento, Srl, Italy

This book is typeset in 10.5 on 12.5 Caslon

The paper used in this book comes from the wood pulp of managed forests. For every tree felled, at least one tree is planted,
thereby renewing natural resources.

A CIP catalogue record for this book is available from the British Library.

In memory of Jackie Grimes (d. 2012),
a lifelong friend and a true inspiration.

Contents

Acknowledgements

Pat

I owe a great many thanks to so many people who have helped enormously.

To Katy McGuinness for her support and creativity in creating this beautiful book.

To Joanne Murphy and her assistant, Líosa Mac Namara, for the wonderful photographs that capture so well all we hoped to achieve; and to Carly and Blondie Horan for their excellent styling.

To Graham Thew for designing the book with skill and flair.

To my entire team at James Whelan Butchers: Ernie, David, Orla, Pat, Alan, Thomas, Hao Liu and Gearoid in Dublin; Stephanie, Frank, Alistair, Harry, Eamon, George, Karl, Owen , Nigel, Trish, Helen, Laura, Lina, Liga, Iveta, Arunas, Helena, Cathy, Dolores, Joan, Francis, Lorraine, Tony, Paul and Jimmy in Clonmel.

Also a special mention to Karl Ryan.

To Simon Pratt and all the team in Avoca, and to Helen King and everyone in Bord Bia who have been a huge inspiration.

To Nichola Beresford and Lorraine McGinniss for their support.

To Nicki Howard, Catherine Gough, Teresa Daly and everyone at Gill & Macmillan – it's been a pleasure working with you.

To my family and friends for their love and patience.

And, finally, to all our loyal customers across Ireland who have made James Whelan Butchers the success it is, thank you.

Katy

My thanks to Pat Whelan for giving me the opportunity to work with him on the book – it's been a serious learning curve (and lots of fun!).

To Rebecca Rowe for being an amazing commis chef and peerless organiser.

To Caroline Kennedy and Maeve Guthrie for their time and chopping skills.

And to Felim, Esme, Talulla, Milo, Ellie and – mustn't forget – Marley Doodle Dunne for being such enthusiastic eaters of beef over the many months of recipe-testing.

Preface

In Ireland, we have the best climate in the world for growing beef.
The combination of abundant rainfall, relatively warm summers
and mild winters makes for ideal grass growing. So we can
console ourselves, as we wake up to yet another 'soft' day, that
at least our growing season is longer and our grass lusher than in
any other country.

The luxuriant green pastures of Ireland, and the good
husbandry practised by our farmers, are responsible for the
world-class quality of Irish beef. Sometimes I think we take this
for granted, when really we should be pausing and taking time to
celebrate this naturally superior product.

In some parts of the world, beef cattle are reared mainly
indoors, fed on concentrates and given steroids and growth
hormones to enhance their yield. In other places, if the climate
is inhospitable to good-quality grass, cattle are reared on dirt. In
these countries, grass-fed beef is a premium product that sells at
a premium price. Yet here in Ireland, grass-fed beef is the norm
– just look around you the next time you're driving through the
Irish countryside and you'll see what I mean. The factory farms
that dominate the landscape in other parts of the world simply
don't exist here. Instead, the rolling green pastures of our farms
are populated by dairy cows and beef cattle munching away on
the goodness of nature's bounty. The milk and beef that's sold in
Ireland today comes from these animals, in much the same way
that it has for thousands of years.

In Ireland, our beef cattle are typically outside for eight months
of the year – so it's just as well that they don't seem to mind the
rain. Only in the winter months, from November to February, do
we bring them inside, and feed them hay and silage, topped up
with a ration of barley, beet pulp, maize and molasses. Thanks

to an excellent diet and superior husbandry, Irish beef has an unparalleled worldwide reputation for excellence.

On our own farm, Garrentemple, near Clonmel in County Tipperary, we raise Angus, Hereford and Wagyu cattle, hardy breeds suited to outdoor rearing. We are blessed to be able to rear our cattle on beautiful pastures overlooked by the Comeragh and Galtee mountains and the majestic Slievenamon, named after the faerie women of ancient legend who enchanted the warrior Finn Mac Cumhaill. There are only a few animals per acre and we go to great lengths to ensure that they have a good quality of life. Natural outdoor rearing is intrinsically healthier for the animal than being raised indoors.

The health benefits to the cattle of being grass-fed are passed on to us when we eat their meat, which is rich in omega 3, vitamin E, antioxidants and the exceptional polyunsaturated marvels that are the omega-6 fats, CLAs (conjugated linoleic acids), which may help to prevent cancer. Eating grass also means that the cattle lay down an intramuscular marbling of fat, which is part of what helps to make the beef taste so good.

Of course, best practice in animal husbandry is just one part of the cycle that brings good meat to our table. For that meat to taste wonderful, there are other equally important steps along the way.

A good stockman – or woman – knows when the time is right for the animal to be slaughtered; it's a skill that takes years to perfect. It's to do with what we call the 'confirmation' – a certain straightness of the back – and an assessment that the animal has laid down exactly the right amount of fat. The most valuable part of the animal is the hindquarter, and so from a business point of view it is part of the farmer's job to assess when the animal has reached its optimum weight and maximum potential.

When that time comes at Garrentemple, we bring our cattle in small social groups to open barns that are only thirty metres away from our own abattoir on the farm. They rest there overnight with generous bedding of loose straw, the freedom to exercise and copious amounts of water.

We treat each animal in a respectful and humane way to minimise stress. As well as wanting to show respect to the animal, this traditional approach to slaughter is good for the meat – relaxed cattle make for better beef. In contrast, an industrial approach geared towards profit margins above all else might involve cattle travelling a significant distance from farm to abattoir, and might not allow the time to ensure that the animals do not suffer stress. The artisan approach is practised by many good cattle farmers all over Ireland, and is one of the reasons for the superb quality of Irish beef.

At Garrentemple, our meat is hung and dry-aged in the traditional way in our own cold rooms adjacent to the abattoir. For our Angus and Hereford cattle, which are slaughtered at around eighteen months and produce small carcasses, the optimum length of hanging is between fourteen and twenty-one days, depending on the cut. For other breeds it can be longer or shorter. Not all the beef sold in Ireland is dry-aged, as this process is more costly in terms of both the time involved and the weight lost in the process, but I believe that meat aged in this way has a richer, more intense flavour and I will continue to follow this approach.

As a fifth-generation butcher on my mother's side of the family, I've grown up understanding that the relationship between butcher and customer is based on trust. It's a business, of course, in the sense that it revolves around a transaction in which money changes hands, but to me it is so much more than that. It is a privilege and an honour to be respected and trusted enough to purvey a product that someone is going to eat.

The relationship between butcher and customer is one in which the parties get to meet regularly, often several times a week. As a butcher, you build up a great familiarity with the customer and their family. You pick up on their likes and dislikes, and you become a part of their world, getting involved in their everyday life as well as the celebrations that happen in their homes – the birthdays and communions and anniversaries and special visits. Butchers are not chefs, but we are there to make suggestions for quick, easy-to-prepare meals that suit busy lives, and as a source of advice and recipes when a customer decides to try a cut that they haven't cooked with before. And although I derive great pleasure from helping my customers to select a majestic cut of rib on the bone for roasting, or a tender whole fillet, I get just as much satisfaction from introducing them to cuts such as shin and skirt, to short ribs and hanger, which give so much flavour and are such excellent value.

In an animal carcass that weighs 520LB-550LB, there are two fillets, each weighing only four or five pounds. In respecting the animal that we have slaughtered, it is part of my philosophy that we should not waste any part of the animal, and so it's very important to me that we make the most of the rest of the carcass – using every bit of it in a celebration of what's become fashionably known as 'nose-to-tail eating'. At home, my family and I enjoy eating the lesser-known cuts just as much as we do the more familiar ones. They are just as tasty, if you know how to cook them. Many supermarkets now offer little choice beyond steak and mince, and I think that over the past few decades the knowledge of what to do with the less familiar cuts has been lost. That's one of the reasons I wanted to write this book, to share the recipes and tips I have accumulated over the years, so that everyone can learn to enjoy the rich diversity of wonderful meals that can be prepared using the best of Irish beef.

I hope you enjoy trying out the recipes as much as Katy McGuinness and I have enjoyed putting them together for you.

Pat Whelan, Clonmel
October 2013

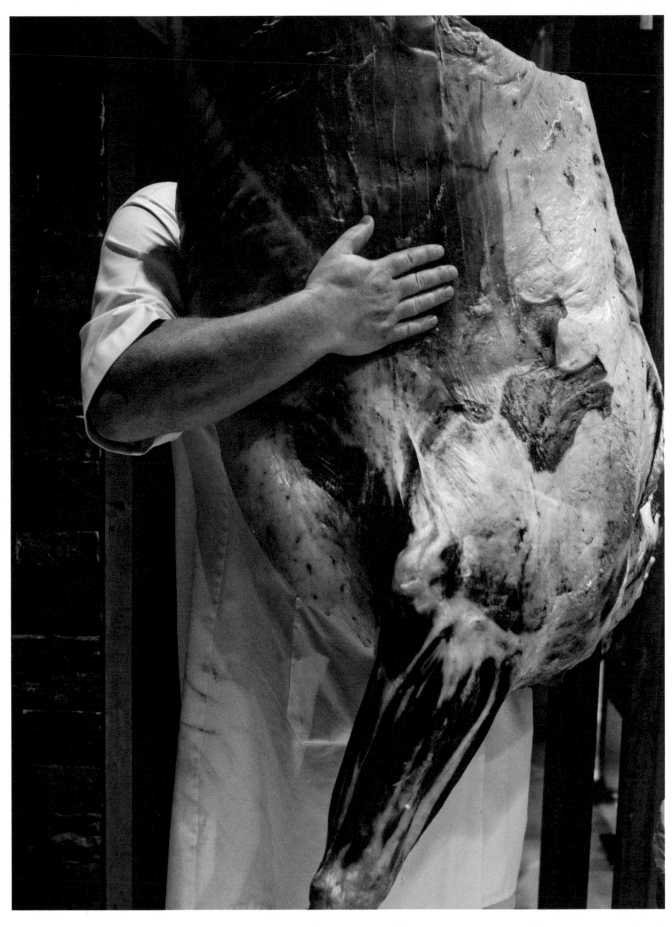

Introduction
Irish Beef: A World-Class Natural Product

In January 2013, chefs from around the world competed at the prestigious Bocuse d'Or international culinary competition, held in the French city of Lyon and regarded as the Olympics of the food world. Irish beef was selected from all the beef submitted for consideration as the principal meat with which the chefs were to work. It was chosen on the basis of its being grass-fed, produced using sustainable farming methods, and of world-class quality, flavour and tenderness. Only the very finest ingredients are selected for this rigorous competition, and it was a great honour for Irish beef farmers to have the quality of the meat they produce vindicated at such an important forum.

What Makes Irish Beef so Good?

Having worked with Irish beef all my life, I believe that there are five main reasons why it is a world-class natural product.

The People

Cattle have been important in Ireland for thousands of years, and in times past a person's wealth was measured in terms of how many cattle they owned. The Irish word for a road – *bóthar* – literally means cow path, wide enough for two cattle to pass each other. A *'boreen'*, or little road, was only wide enough for one animal.

Irish agricultural production today is based on a network of over one hundred and twenty thousand small farms. These holdings have been passed from generation to generation over the centuries, along with the craft and the love of livestock farming. Cattle are cherished in Ireland; they are at the heart of Irish farming, and farmers take great pride in the continual improvement of their stock. The uniqueness of the Irish smallholding, and the knowledge that passes down through families along with the land, is at the core of what makes Irish beef wonderful.

The Place

Ireland's temperate climate benefits from the gentle influence of the Gulf Stream, which brings warming waters from the Gulf of Mexico to northern Europe. Abundant rainfall is the most obvious evidence of this, making green pastures the mainstay of Irish agriculture. A further reason for the richness of the country's farming tradition is a secret resource underground: the centre of Ireland lies above the largest continuous stretch of carboniferous limestone in Europe. This limestone gives Ireland's farmland excellent drainage, and its grasses a rich source of calcium and other nutrients – in other words, perfect grazing conditions.

The Tradition

While climate and geology are important, history and culture have a place too. Cattle have been a part of the Irish landscape for over five thousand years, and their presence has helped shape the political, social and cultural fabric of the country. Traditionally, cows were the unit of currency and owning cattle was the measure of status. Cattle raids, in which neighbouring communities captured each other's cattle, were a distinctive part of Irish life – a social institution – for a thousand years. One of the most famous tales in Irish mythology concerns the Cattle Raid of Cooley, in which Queen Medbh sought to capture the great brown bull, defended by the famous warrior Cú Chulainn.

The Cattle

Traditional native Irish breeds such as the Kerry and the Dexter were central to the herds of ancient Ireland. At Farmleigh, the state still grazes a full herd of Kerry cows on

WATERFORD CASTLE

°°°

DEXTER BEEF DINNER

14th SEPTEMBER 2012

°°°

OXTAIL CROQUETTE *with* ROASTING JUICES

CASTLE SMOKED WOODSTOWN OYSTER, BRAISED BRISKET *&* MADEIRA

CONSOMMÉ *with* BONE MARROW

DUNMORE EAST MONKFISH, AUTUMN BABY VEGETABLES, MUSSELS *&* BEEF JUS

TRIO OF DEXTER BEEF, DAUBE, FILLET TARTARE *&* ROAST RIB

BLAA PUDDING

°°°

The menu is based around a traditional Irish breed of house cow. We purchased a whole animal and have included various cuts of meat in each course. By doing this we are putting the emphasis back on old Irish breeds of cattle.

HEAD CHEF MICHAEL QUINN

the pastures of Dublin's Phoenix Park, offering a rare glimpse into this living heritage. The Dexter is today very popular among smallholders the world over, and is enjoying something of a resurgence in Ireland. It is one of the smallest breeds and is a very productive dual-purpose animal, producing both high-quality milk and meat. In 2012, Michael Quinn, then head chef at Waterford Castle, served a six-course dinner celebrating the breed – Dexter beef was used in every single course bar the pudding. The Irish Moiled, another dual-purpose breed, comes in an attractive range of speckled red and white colours and is native to Northern Ireland. Like the Kerry and Dexter, it can survive on very poor pastures, and produces beef with great marbling and flavour.

With the coming of the agricultural revolution in the eighteenth century, Ireland's cattle breeds and the appearance of the Irish countryside were to change forever. The oak forests that had once covered most of the country were cut down and fields, enclosed by hedges, took their place. This new form of farming relied on high-quality pasture, and breeds such as Shorthorn, Hereford and Angus were introduced from across the water. Irish breeders quickly excelled with these new breeds, and exported large numbers of them back to their homeland. With this new productivity, Ireland became a major exporter of beef. It's a role that has continued right up to the present day.

At first, exports of live cattle were common, but exports of fresh bone-in beef to the Smithfield markets of Victorian London began in the early 1890s. Today Ireland is a centre of excellence for many breeds and is an important source of genetic improvement for farmers around the world. Ireland now exports about 90% of its beef output, making it the northern hemisphere's largest net exporter of beef. Ireland has a human population of approximately 4.5 million, yet is estimated to produce enough beef annually to feed 28 million people.

The Grass

At the heart of the Irish beef success story is our national herd of approximately one million suckler cows. Almost 75% of the national herd calves in the spring, with calves generally spending the first six to ten months suckling their mothers at pasture. They reap the benefit of the longest grass-growing season in Europe, grazing a continuous diet of fresh grass and clover. By the time of slaughter almost 90% of their diet will have been grass – by far the highest percentage for any cattle in Europe.

Scientific studies show that grass is a more natural diet for beef cattle than grain. Grass-fed beef has a more even distribution of fat – marbling – which makes eating it a more enjoyable sensory experience. Grass-fed beef also has higher levels of vitamin A and beta-carotene, giving Irish beef a rich burgundy colour. In addition, a higher ratio of omega 3 fatty acids and CLAs have been linked by a growing number of scientific studies to health benefits in humans, such as lowering cholesterol and reducing cancer risk. Nowhere is the adage 'you are what you eat' more true – the consumer who eats grass-fed beef gains a significant health advantage.

Family History

The tradition and craft of butchering has been in my family for five generations. My father, James Whelan, is a farmer's son from Dungarvan, Co. Waterford and my mother, Joan Scanlon, a butcher's daughter from Cappoquin, also in Co. Waterford. When they met, my mother was working in her family's butcher's shop. Clonmel was the nearest big town for both of them – it was roughly equidistant from their two home towns – and when they married, they bought an existing butcher's shop in the town and made their home above the shop.

At the outset, all the meat they sold in the shop came from their home family farms, but they soon established their own farm, at Garrentemple. My father continues to farm the land and, as I spend more and more time with him, I have come to appreciate that he has forgotten more about farming and livestock than I will ever know. I like the sense of continuity that comes from working with my father, and it reinforces my view that my role is that of guardian of the land for my children, with the responsibility to look after it well for the future.

My mother and father worked together, and she set up what's known as a 'country business' – a simple mobile shop. She used to fill the boot of the car (the first I remember was an Opel Rekord) and set off into the hinterland to sell our meat door to door. One day she'd go to Clooneen near Fethard and the next it might be Ballymacarberry or Rathcormack. It was a great service for people living out in the country who didn't have their own car or found it difficult to get in to town, and it established a tangible connection with many people who lived locally. She'd keep a 'book', as a lot of the sales she made would be on credit (or 'tick' as it was known in those days), and then when her customers' creamery cheques came in they would visit the shop and settle their account. The foundations of the business we have today were built in those days.

When you grow up in a family business, it's more than a business – it's an extension of who you are – and you're involved from a very early age. Because we lived over the shop, I'd be in and out on my way to and from school, absorbing the atmosphere and connecting with the day's routine. I was helping out on the farm and in the shop from when I was about six or seven. It might have only been something as small as stopping cattle at a gate, or labelling the turkeys at Christmastime, but you were still part of it.

I have fond memories of the people who worked in the business with my parents, whether in the shop or the abattoir or on the farm. Some families have been working with us for generations and there's a real sense of common purpose that goes hand in hand with the carrying on of traditions, and a shared understanding as to how things are done – and done properly. It's important to me to have that continuity, and the mutual respect that develops over time. When I was growing up we always fed all the men who worked with us their dinner – in the middle of the day – in the dining room at the back of the shop. The kitchen and dining room were behind the shop, and behind that again was the slaughterhouse. It was good plain food; I used to like the braised brisket and corned beef, and the spiced beef around Christmastime. Feeding the people who worked with us was a form of nurturing, a pause in the middle of the day to acknowledge the value of each person's contribution.

At Christmas we'd send parcels of smoked ham and spiced beef to customers and their families in the UK, and my mother would melt wax over a flame and pour it onto the knot of the string that tied up the parcel. I often think that the online business I've developed over the last decade has its roots in the same principles – it just has a bigger reach. Many of our customers order from us regularly; repeat business is the best endorsement you can have. There's still plenty of demand for the smoked ham and spiced beef.

In the 1970s, Clonmel's first shopping centre opened. There would be late night shopping and six-day trading – we were used to a half day on Thursday – and my parents decided that this was the way of the future, and opened a second shop in the shopping centre. I remember cycling between the two premises with legs of lamb and parcels of beef when one of the shops ran out. The shopping centre opened up the town to outsiders and was hugely successful. People really embraced that radical change. We opened our first Dublin shop in Monkstown in 2010, and this year we opened a second in Rathcoole, but our shop in Clonmel continues to serve the loyal customers who have been coming to us since the 1960s.

On the Craft of Butchery

There has long been a shyness, almost a taboo, about butchery. To me it is an art, a craft, something to be celebrated, and I want to tell people about it. I think people have a right to know what's involved, and the more transparent we make what we do, the better. There's a tremendous beauty in the English language. We have been blessed with an abundant tongue based on rich, ancient foundations. We have an instrument of expression that when used correctly can work incredible magic. Words can make us fall in love, do things we don't want to do, create mental pictures and even stir up emotions we didn't even know existed. There is power in words and yet we are often lazy, assuming that some subjects don't deserve a richer word currency.

While the word 'passion' is often bandied about and overused these days, it should be fully applied to butchers. When I recruit trainees or qualified butchers to work with me, I look for people with an ardent interest. I want people who border on the obsessive, because then and only then will we have a chance at creating a healthy legacy. I am often asked if I 'minded' taking over the family business! It always amazes me that anyone would think I was obligated or forced in some way to follow in my parents' footsteps. I genuinely love every part of the business.

I had butchery in my blood and for me it was a natural step, so in some ways I was simply fulfilling my purpose and calling. While I'm thankful that I have such a strong ancestral link to raising stock for food and the noble craft of butchery, I firmly believe that it would have been the perfect job for me had I no family background in butchery.

Many people miss the fundamental reasons why someone might want to take up this trade. I often find myself standing at a fence in the dew-drenched, quiet early morning, marvelling at the wonder of the animals I rear and the link they provide between the land and us. While I take great care in raising them, and enjoy their intrinsic, melancholic majesty, I am also starkly aware of their ultimate purpose. These gracious, primal mammals provide us with food that keeps us healthy and makes us strong. I acknowledge the responsibility of ensuring that we make the most of their surrender. As a butcher it is up to me to find out everything I can about the animal and the nutrition it can provide. I am responsible for making sure that every part of the animal that is a source of nourishment can be used as such. It is up to me to know how to cook any cut of meat, nose-to-tail and including the bones, and to have personal experience of that so I can pass on my knowledge. It is a calling, a purpose, and so much more than just a job. It is in this kind of thinking that one finds the joy.

Besides the cerebral there is also the physical. Part of the work of a butcher is not pretty. It is bloody, heavy and serious. That neatly tied, attractive little package, or the ruby red fillet of steak that tempts you from behind the gleaming glass of a butcher's counter, was once part of a large and unwieldy carcass; and it took a deft combination of skill and art to produce such an aesthetically appealing result.

The Philosophy

I've been immersed in the world of meat since I was a child. Over the years, I've learned the skills of the farmer, the stockman, the slaughterman, the butcher, the shopkeeper and the businessman. I believe fundamentally that every one of those skills is required to ensure the successful journey of high-quality meat from farm to fork.

My father used to bring me with him when he went to the mart, and I would watch him buying cattle. I observed the honour system, and saw that transactions are dependent on trust. Money often changes hands some time after the deal is struck, but I have never heard of a seller having any difficulty in getting paid. Respect and sincerity are an integral part of the way business is done; there's an 'again' in it – an expectation that down the line you will be dealing with each other again and it's in everyone's interests to ensure that a long-term relationship has firm foundations, that it is based on honesty and integrity.

The notion of the 'again' informs good practice at every stage in the artisan method of beef production. If everyone involved in the food chain that brings meat from the land to the table takes pride in their work and strives for excellence at every step on the way, our food will be of the highest possible quality and our health will reap the rewards.

In the various roles that I fulfil, from farmer to butcher, I have taken a conscious decision always to choose the right way, and not to opt for the time- or money-saving shortcut. In practical terms, this means that we do not over-crowd our cattle on the farm; we treat them humanely and keep their stress levels to a minimum; we respect their carcass and use it efficiently, without waste; we dry-age their meat in a traditional way; and we butcher it carefully. There is no room for sentiment – none of the cattle has a name, for instance – but there is huge respect.

One of the ways in which we pay respect to the animal is by using every bit of its carcass. I think of this as a way of honouring the sacrifice that the animal has made. It's common these days to go into a supermarket and see no beef on offer bar generic 'steak', 'casserole beef' and 'mince'. This way of selling meat is responsible for the de-skilling of butchers, whose role is limited to preparing packages rather than a variety of cuts to optimise the whole carcass. It makes me sad to see this disconnection between the animal and the meat, and to see the role of the butcher so diminished, and I have made it my business in my own small way that I and the butchers in my shops introduce our customers to cuts of beef that they will never see in a supermarket and to teach them how to use them. I cherish equally all the various cuts of meat that the animal has to offer, and aim to eat them in proportion, so that over the course of a period of time I will have eaten every bit of nourishment from the bounty that the animal has to offer. To eat only the premium cuts, as they are known – fillet, striploin and rib-eye – is a form of asset stripping. No cut of meat is inferior to any other – there is no ladder of flavour in a hierarchical sense – but the cook does need to know how to handle each cut in order to get the best out of it.

We hold regular butchery classes in our shops and these have become very popular with customers who want to learn the anatomy of the animal and understand more about the meat they cook. I was struck recently when one student who had been listening to me explain my philosophy of eating the whole animal in proportion describe it as the 'democratisation of meat'. She said she felt empowered by what she had learned, inspired to experiment more creatively and confident that she could have better dialogue with her butcher in the future.

From a desire to bring our customers closer to the livestock and help them to understand better the nature of our business, we have developed Beef Bonds, which give the bondholder a share in one of our Angus, Hereford or Wagyu cattle. Each Beef Bond includes the ID number, breed and expected maturity date of the animal to which it is linked. The bonds can be short or long term and, on maturity, the investor takes delivery of various cuts of prime Tipperary beef. Each bondholder is guaranteed a defined return on his or her investment, based on the expected maturity weight of the animal. A long-term maturity bond offers the potential of an additional return if the animal exceeds its expected maturity weight. The Beef Bond is a 'nose to tail' approach to selling beef and affords our customers the opportunity to share the familiar and lesser-known cuts equally.

The Butcher–Customer Relationship

A customer's relationship with their butcher is akin to the relationship they have with their doctor or chemist. People tend to have a pattern around shopping – you can set the clock by some customers – so it's a relationship that builds over time, one that develops each time the customer comes into the shop.

The relationship is born out of trust. A customer has to trust their butcher implicitly, to be confident that they are getting high-quality meat that has been handled properly at every step along the journey from farm to shop. I am saddened by the industrial approach to the sale of meat, which has removed from the food chain that personal relationship between farmer and butcher, and between butcher and customer. It is an impersonal approach that seems to set little store by the skills the butcher has learned over the years, and offers scant connection between the farmer who produces the meat and the shopper who buys it. It's small wonder that so many people don't know what to do when faced with a steak that isn't a fillet or a rib-eye, or are intimidated by the prospect of serving a roast to their family and friends on a Sunday afternoon.

It all goes back to the respect for the animal that lies deep within the psyche of the Irish farmer.

Butchery is a serious business, and beef is more than a commodity to me. As a farmer, I have contributed to creating the life of the animal and I look on it in the same way an artist would look at their painting. I know the animals, not by name, but I know their personalities. I know their mothers, and the gene pool from which they came. It's a business of consequences. You must understand the stock, the slaughtering, the maturation and the butchering in order to be able to stand over the quality and provenance of the meat you sell. When meat is looked at as a commodity, and profit margins dictate what happens to it at every step on the journey from the field to the table, it is not always possible for the seller to be as sure of the quality of what they are selling, nor the customer of what they are buying.

The relationship with the customer is an extension of the sense of responsibility that I view as being such a fundamental part of my job as a butcher. I see our customers as part of the larger family that includes the animals and the people who work with me. I feel that I owe them the same duty of care as I do my own family. Good butchers – and there are many in Ireland – take the trouble to know the journey that each animal makes from farm to fork, and are able to share that information with their customers.

To me, a natural being deserves better than to be treated as an industrial commodity. I am also wholly convinced that the traditional, artisan approach is repaid with meat that is more tender and has better flavour.

A while back I had the pleasure of welcoming Carrie Oliver, the self-confessed 'meat geek' from the USA, to the farm. She demonstrated to me how our grass-fed, artisan meat even smells different from industrial meat; it bears testament to its 'terroir' – the pasture on which it was fed – and the respectful manner of its slaughter, hanging and ageing, in the same way that wine is influenced by the soil and climate in which grows, the manner of its harvest and the care and attention that is given to the process of bringing it to the point of being enjoyed in a glass.

An important part of my job as a butcher is to be a source of advice and knowledge for my customers. It's not just about giving them timings for a special Sunday roast, but also about teaching them how to make the most of the less familiar cuts with which they can eat well every day even if budgets are tight. Most butchers do not purport to be chefs, but the majority are enthusiastic home cooks who take an interest in what their customers are hoping to achieve, and will gladly share recipes and tips. Asking their advice is a way of paying tribute to and acknowledging their skills, and they will also be eager to learn from their customers.

How do you find a good butcher? In the first instance, ask around friends and neighbours. Try out their recommendations. Ask the butcher a few questions about the beef they're selling, and establish how much they know about it – what kind of animal it came from, at what age it was slaughtered and how long it has been hung. Ask where the animal was reared. Ask for bones for your dog – if they don't have any, they're either lacking in generosity of spirit or they're buying in the meat ready prepared and aren't butchering it themselves. The closer you can get to the source of the meat, the better; so look out for butchers whose meat comes from their own family farms. Ask too about the availability of some of the cuts mentioned in this book – are short ribs available, or hanger steak, or shin on the bone? How much notice will they need to get these cuts? If the butcher is open and receptive to this conversation, and gives you the information that you want, you may have found your man – or woman. If you have the time and money, buy a particular cut of steak from several butchers on the same day and cook and compare them. You'll soon figure out which tastes best.

And once you've found a great butcher, never let them go – it's a relationship that will have serious consequences for your future health and well-being!

How to Choose Good-Quality Meat

The best way of ensuring that you always buy good-quality beef is to make friends with your local butcher. While words like 'traceability' sound very bureaucratic, you should be able simply to ask your butcher, 'Where did this come from?' and expect a simple, accurate response.

Beef should be hung after slaughter for a period of two weeks or longer. Hanging beef (dry ageing) gives the enzymes and bacteria in the meat time to start breaking down the fibres, which, in time, makes the meat more tender and gives it more flavour. It helps the meat lose moisture, making it better for cooking. Don't be afraid to ask how long the meat has been hung. Beef from a good-quality, independent butcher is more likely to be worth eating.

However, if you are buying beef and don't have the luxury of dealing with someone you know to be a knowledgeable and trustworthy butcher, here are some tips.

- Look for beef that is a deep ruby red in colour, and has thin creamy-white fat evenly distributed throughout. This marbling enables the beef to 'baste' itself from within during cooking.

- A layer of firm, creamy-white fat around the outside of a nicely marbled joint is a sign of a properly reared, good-quality animal. After it has basted the meat and added flavour during cooking, fat can be drained away or cut off.

- Good-quality, properly hung beef should look dry and be yielding to the touch, but not flabby or without form.

- Some cuts of meat are just naturally more tender than others, regardless of the so-called 'quality'. Meat from areas where there is a lot of muscle use, such as the legs, shoulder and neck, will be tougher than the less-used muscles along the back, such as the rib and loin. The tougher cuts are better for slow cooking and braising.

- If there is packaging, check for any damage. The meat should be cold and wrapped securely.

Breeds

At Garrentemple, we have farmed Aberdeen Angus and Hereford cattle for years. More recently, we have introduced a foundation herd of Wagyu.

Aberdeen Angus

The Aberdeen Angus derives from breeds native to the highlands of Scotland, working animals that were later bred and improved. Originally, the cattle found in the northern regions of Scotland varied in colour and, while many were polled (without horns), some still had horns. The counties from which the breed originates all touch the North Sea, extend inland and have some high or mountainous country. The temperate climate and well-distributed rainfall produces good crops, although the topography is rough. Plenty of grass, plus a nearly ideal temperature for cattle production, has made the area very suitable for some of the greatest improvements that have ever been made in purebred cattle.

During the second half of the eighteenth century, farmers sought to improve the livestock on their farms. They began buying cattle of similar kinds from adjacent areas and crossed the Angus 'doddie' strain with the Buchan 'humlie'. Crossing and re-crossing the strains of cattle eventually led to a distinct breed – the Aberdeen Angus – that was not very different from either type, since the two strains were originally quite similar.

Hugh Watson, of Keillor in the county of Angus, was one of the founders of the breed. At the age of 19, when he started farming, his father gave him six of his best and blackest cows and a bull. That same summer he visited some of the leading Scottish cattle markets and purchased the ten best heifers and the best bull he could find that showed characteristics of the Angus cattle he was striving to breed. The females varied in colour but the bull was black. Watson wanted his herd to be black, so he started selecting in that direction. His favourite bull was Old Jock 126, awarded the number '1' in the first Herd Book. This bull, bred in 1842 and sired by Grey-Breasted Jock 113, was used extensively in the herd between 1843 and 1852. Watson also had a very famous cow called Old Granny 125, which produced a total of twenty-nine calves, eleven of which were registered in the Herd Book.

Other early contributors to the breed included Lord Panmure, who established a herd of polled cattle in 1835 and not only operated a private herd but also encouraged his tenants to breed good 'doddies'; and William Fullerton, who began to breed cattle in 1833, and whose Aberdeen cow Black Meg is sometimes referred to as the founder of the breed, since more cattle trace to her than to any other female used in the origin of the breed. She is the only cow to surpass Old Granny in this respect.

Hereford

The Hereford breed originated in Herefordshire, England, nearly three hundred years ago, and Benjamin Tompkins is considered to be its primary founder. Farmers developed the Hereford to fill the need for a beef cow that could efficiently convert grass to pounds of beef, and do it at a profit. The breed was selected and bred for its natural ability to grow and gain on grass and grain; and also for its hardiness, early maturation and high reproduction rates.

Herefords in the 1700s and early 1800s were much larger than they are today. Mature Herefords could weigh up to three thousand pounds. Since then, the Hereford breed has gone through many changes, and today's Herefords are optimum-size cattle that suit today's industry. They are less extreme in size and weight, weighing on average about a thousand to twelve hundred pounds, which results in quality and efficiency.

Herefords were exported to the USA during the nineteenth century and soon became very popular, proving they could survive rough ranching conditions, extreme temperatures and poor forage, while continuing to improve the quality of their beef. For these reasons, Hereford cattle were given the name 'the Great Improvers', a title that still stands today.

It was an American who was responsible for developing the polled Hereford breed. In 1898, an Iowa cattleman by the name of Warren Gammon saw an exposition of 'naturally hornless' Herefords at the Trans-Mississippi World's Fair in Omaha, Nebraska. He set out to 'fix' the hornless trait using a bull named Giant and eleven females.

The black Aberdeen Angus and the red and white Hereford continue to be the benchmark against which all other breeds are measured. Both breeds are naturally robust and take on a coat in winter as they are used to wintering outside. They are small-framed animals and come to beef quickly, at around eighteen months.

Angus and Hereford cattle produce terrific meat. The small carcass, muscle profile and capacity to develop intramuscular marbling make them perfect for steak cuts. They are breeds that do well both indoors and out, and they are naturally docile, with a gentle temperament that makes them easy to manage. They are also naturally polled, so they don't need to be de-horned, which can be stressful for an animal. One of the principal tenets on our farm at Garrentemple is to cause as little stress as possible to our animals, as stress has a negative impact on the quality of the meat.

Wagyu

Mother Nature is a great teacher. When it comes to growing and rearing food, the laws of sowing and reaping, of getting your hands dirty, adding time, waiting, and then waiting some more for a successful outcome, is a good analogy for life in general. Despite our love of instant gratification, Nature refuses to bow down and, regardless of how fast we want something, remains beautifully consistent.

If we want real and authentic over artificial and synthetic, there can be no compromise – a lesson brought home to me as I consider my herd of Wagyu. What started as a project has become a passion.

The story started when I discovered Wagyu beef on a visit to Japan in 2008. The trip was organised by Bord Bia, whose staff have always been a huge help to me. They encourage innovation and have created an environment that helps food producers to step outside their comfort zone. They have encouraged me to look at my business and consider ways in which I can add value in unexpected areas. Their innovation programme gets Irish farmers and food producers behind the scenes and connects them with owner-managers and producers around the world. The level of access that they are able to facilitate is very impressive.

The term 'Wagyu' refers to several different breeds of cattle, some of which are similar to Angus in that they were also bred for working. *Wa* means 'Japan', and *gyu* means 'cow' – so Wagyu means 'cow of Japan'. Kobe is the region of Japan where some of the specific bloodlines of Wagyu are bred; it's the equivalent of Tipperary in Ireland. The terms Wagyu and Kobe are often used interchangeably.

In Japan, I was very taken with how the Japanese eat meat; their attitude is reverential. They buy meat by the gram and eat it boiled in oil rather than fried. Meat with a high fat score is greatly sought after – the higher the fat content, the better the meat. Wagyu cattle have a natural capacity to develop concentrated intramuscular marbling, a tendency that can be exaggerated with diet and husbandry. Because of the marbling, Wagyu meat is incredibly succulent. It has a buttery, more generous taste than other beef, and the fat melts at room temperature. Wagyu beef is sometimes referred to as the foie gras of beef and is much sought after as a culinary delicacy. The fat is mono-unsaturated, and has the capacity to break down bad HDL (high-density lipoprotein) cholesterol – another of the reasons why it is so revered by the Japanese.

Having had the Wagyu experience in Japan, I returned home to Clonmel wanting to bring Wagyu to my shop and my customers. However, the idea of importing beef from Japan didn't sit easily with my home-grown, local food ethos, which I believe in as strongly today as I always have. Our family business has been in existence for over forty years, and this ethos is without doubt one of the reasons for our longevity. What doesn't come from my own farm comes from farmers I know personally. Being able to visit their farms and build relationships with them is an important pillar of what I do and who I am, and it enables me to stand over everything we sell. This would not be possible if we used a supplier from Japan – and that was before we even considered the financial cost. I had to find another way.

The prospect of starting a Wagyu herd in Ireland seemed like a bridge too far, but my interest had been piqued, and I joined the World Wagyu Association online. I discovered that some farmers in Australia were breeding Wagyu out to Angus (i.e. crossing them), with positive results. Given that I already had an intimate knowledge of the Angus, I began to feel that this was something I should explore further.

First, I studied the genetic structure and gene pool of both the Angus and the Wagyu, which are aesthetically very similar. It was quite exciting to think that by crossing the two breeds I would be able to grow on the Wagyu a little bigger to get the fat score right. In Japan, the cattle are reared indoors, massaged and fed a by-product of sake manufacture; the alcohol enhances their appetite. I didn't quite see how that would work in Garrentemple. But I discovered that in Australia they were using parallel farming methods to those that we use with the Angus cattle at home in Tipperary.

Then I went to Australia, where I saw Wagyu reared outdoors on grass, with an adjusted diet to encourage the development of intramuscular marbling. I could see that this could work in Ireland, where we have even better growing conditions, and I was excited by the prospect of trying to establish a foundation herd of Wagyu cattle at home. I think it was the potential to innovate, to create something new that would add value to the farm for generations, that really got me thinking.

Back in Ireland, I set about making the dream a reality. The first step was to cross the Wagyu with our own Angus. I deliberately sought out gene pools that promised a docile temperament, and animals that were naturally polled (without horns) and came to beef quickly. Our vet performed artificial insemination, using imported straws of Wagyu semen and our own female breeding stock, and we waited with bated breath for the first calves to be born nine months later.

The frame of the Angus is small, but Wagyu typically have a low birth weight and there were no calving problems. When they are born, the Wagyu look tiny, but they are very robust, come into their own quickly and grow fast. It was a very proud moment for me to see the first calves being born.

The next step was to breed full-blood Wagyu. We imported fertilised embryos from Japan, carefully chosen to avoid inbreeding, which is crucial in the foundation of a herd. The embryos were implanted into surrogates and 75% of that first batch took – a very high rate. The foundations of the full-blood family that derives from those embryos comprise eleven different strains of blood in the pure Wagyu. It gives me a great sense of achievement when I see the names of their Japanese parents on the ear tags of Wagyu cattle born in Tipperary.

As far as possible, I have tried to recreate the Wagyu's natural environment at Garrentemple. The farm and the environment in which an animal is reared are as important as its breeding when it comes to producing quality beef. The pasture that the Wagyu graze in the shadow of the Comeragh Mountains, and the fact that the farm is eight hundred feet above sea level, simulates their natural habitat in Japan.
We are still in the process of developing a foundation herd that will bring a regular supply of Wagyu beef to the Irish market. There is plenty of trial and error involved, but it's exciting to be in at the start of something that I believe is truly special. Having visited many vineyards on my travels, I can compare the process to that of making a new, unique wine. For me, it's an opportunity to develop something recognised as a world-class product in an Irish context, and to make a lasting contribution – something that will be sustainable for future generations.

The Wagyu represent a great deal to me, not least the lesson about time and patience. They are also a personal achievement and a testament to how ideals and values can be preserved without compromising progress.

Food Culture in Ireland and Irish Artisan Food Producers

I have holidayed in France many times and one of the things that I love most is that every village square has its own independently run baker, butcher and grocer. There isn't a multiple in sight. And the quality is always pretty good, and sometimes outstanding.
For me, as a butcher and shopkeeper, it's comforting to see the French protect their skills. If one butcher closes for the holidays, there'll be a sign in the window recommending his customers visit another in the vicinity. It's a kind of 'co-opetition', and it must stack up commercially – otherwise it wouldn't happen.

I see that kind of collaborative endeavour coming back: that there are signs of a resurgence of the desire for a sense of community cropping up all over the country. Over the past year, I have had the pleasure of visiting several regional food festivals and have been heartened by the enthusiasm of the members of the food community in Ireland to work together towards a common and mutually supportive purpose.

TIPPERARY LONG TABLE DINNER

∘∘∘

CAHIR CASTLE
27TH AUGUST 2008

∘∘∘

ROASTED AUBERGINE INVOLTINI *with* BAYLOUGH FARMHOUSE SMOKED CHEDDAR, TIPPERARY CREAM CHEESE *&* CASHEL BLUE

THYME AND BLACK PUDDING TIPPERARY SAUSAGE SKEWER
with RED PEPPER RELISH

CAHIR CASTLE BREAD

BARBECUED LEG OF TIPPERARY LAMB *with* HERB CRUST *&* REDCURRANT JELLY

CIDER-GLAZED SMOKED HAM

CREAMY POTATO *&* LEEK GRATIN

WALDORF SALAD

COUSCOUS *with* ROASTED VEGETABLES

GREEN LEAF *and* HERB SALAD

TIPPERARY GLORY

TIPPERARY CHEESE BOARD

COFFEE/TEA *with* SHORTBREAD COOKIE

∘∘∘

TIPPERARY FOOD PRODUCERS' MENU

°°°

LONG TABLE DINNER, EMBASSY OF IRELAND, BRUSSELS, BELGIUM. 25TH JUNE 2013

PREPARED & COOKED BY BARBARA RUSSELL, RUSSELL CATERING,
CLONMEL, & SARAH BAKER, CLOUGHJORDAN HOUSE & COOKERY SCHOOL

°°°

DRINKS RECEPTION

THE APPLE FARM FRUIT PUNCH

BULMERS CHILLED LIGHT APPLE *and* PEAR CIDERS

CANAPÉS

HOT & COLD SMOKED GOATSBRIDGE TROUT
MOUSSE *with* CAVIAR

SHEEPWALK FARM ORGANIC LAMB KOFTA *served with*
CROSSOGUE PRESERVES RED ONION MARMALADE

COOLEENEY FARMHOUSE CHEESE *served with*
O'DONNELL'S CRISPS

VARIETY OF 100% IRISH PORK HERB & GARLIC
COCKTAIL SAUSAGES

STARTER

PIEDMONT CARPACCIO FILLET *with* ROCKET LETTUCE
& MUSTARD SAUCE

MAINS

CROWE'S FARM JUNIPER BERRY SMOKED LOIN OF
BACON *with* HONEY & MUSTARD GLAZE FROM
'THE SCULLERY'

HERB CRUSTED LEG OF WHELAN'S LAMB STUFFED
with INCH HOUSE BLACK PUDDING
& REDCURRANT SAUCE

'RED NOSE' WINE SELECTION

SALADS

MINTED POTATO SALAD

GREEN SALAD *with* CROZIER CASHEL BLUE DRESSING

BABY BEETS TOSSED IN CHERVIL *and* TOASTED
SESAME SEEDS

DESSERT

MAG'S HOME BAKERY MINI MERINGUE *with*
CROSSOGUE WHISKEY COFFEE CURD

SERVED *with* BOULABAN SALTED CARAMEL
ICE CREAM

LOUGH DERG CHOCOLATE *and* HICKEY BAKERY
BRIOCHE BREAD & BUTTER PUDDING

CHEESE PLATE

ALL SERVED *with* OATEN CRACKERS FROM
'THE COOKIE JAR'.

CASHEL BLUE

COOLEENEY GORTNAMONA GOAT'S CHEESE

COOLEENEY DUNBARRA CHEESE

PETIT FOURS

CHOCOLATE CHIP MINI COOKIES

LOUGH DERG CHOCOLATES

CHOCOLATE BISCUIT CAKE *from* THE TIPPERARY
KITCHEN

'PONÁIRE' COFFEE

In our shop in Clonmel I have always sold food produced locally, and am amazed by the amount of locally produced food that has come to the fore, making the option to eat locally a real, sustainable choice. The kitchen table in my house is where we try everything out and my family is the taste council. That's how we select what goes into the shop.

I really enjoy the ability to connect with producers and influence how they produce. I like the fact that I only need to pick up the phone or drive a short distance to discuss things with them directly. It's something that I've developed in Tipperary, where we have such an abundance of wonderful local produce.

A few years back, out of that desire for local producers to come together, came the first Tipperary Long Table dinner, which we held in Cahir Castle in 2008. The whole menu was sourced from Tipperary.

We invited all the producers and stakeholders, including local government representatives, and I consider myself very lucky that the initiative has resulted in not only commercial links but also great friendships with other food producers, which have enriched my life inordinately. As a group, we take pride in each others' successes as well as our own.

Out of that first Long Table Dinner was born the Tipperary Food Producers' Network, the philosophy of which is that of the Irish *meitheal*, a coming together in the name of a common enterprise for the good of all. We share the experience and we all learn from it. It has grown into something extraordinary. People co-operate with their delivery runs, so if someone has space on a van going to Dublin, they'll let the others know; and out of that have come all sorts of cross-merchandising initiatives. We have an annual dinner and we meet regularly; it is a vibrant organisation of which I am proud to be the chair. (For details of these food producers, see the Appendix, page 232.) In June 2013, we held our first international longtable dinner in the Embassy of Ireland in Brussels to celebrate the Irish presidency of the EU. The dinner was organised by Tipperary man Karl Ryan, who works as a parliamentary assistant in the city.

What we have done in Tipperary is starting to happen all over the country as bands of producers come together to promote the idea of supporting their local food community. To me, Ballymaloe House in Co. Cork is at the epicentre of great Irish cooking, and a shining beacon of inspiration for the whole Irish food community. Myrtle and Darina Allen have pioneered a style of cooking that uses seasonal ingredients to produce great-tasting, simple, home-grown, clean food – the kind we should all cherish. It is food with integrity, which is revered the world over; and something of which we should all be very proud. Because of Ballymaloe's positive influence on the local community, west Cork now has a vibrant food culture that is known and respected internationally.

The Slow Food Praesidia are great at protecting rare food products, but I think the common things need to be protected too, so that people have a real choice in where they shop and what they eat. It makes such a difference in a community to have proper shops – not just supermarkets – with a decent variety of locally produced products.

Irish producers have been developing some wonderful, innovative products in recent years. Irish rapeseed oil is replacing imported olive oil in many kitchens. Our cheesemakers are superb – you will find recipes in this book using Crozier Blue, Hegarty's Cheddar, Coolea, Desmond and Cratloe Hills – and are gaining recognition around the world. Toonsbridge, also in Co. Cork, is even producing mozzarella and ricotta from buffalo milk, and very good it is too. Highbank Orchard Syrup is a fabulous organic product, made from apples, that can be used in many recipes as an alternative to honey or maple syrup. My neighbours at Crowe's Farm in Tipperary make a terrific pancetta from their outdoor-bred pigs, while my friends at Goatsbridge in Co. Kilkenny produce Irish trout caviar, which is as good as anything that comes from a sturgeon and features on menus in some of the country's best restaurants. And of course we have an abundance of seasonal fruit and vegetables.

All over Ireland, food producers are bringing new products to market. If we could all go about our food shopping in a more considered way, and make the effort to seek out local alternatives to the imported products that we throw into our supermarket trolleys without a second thought, we could go a long way towards developing and building an Irish regional food culture of which the whole country can be proud.

Cuts

Forequarter

4   **Back rib** – best boned and rolled for slow or pot-roasting.

7   **Top rib** – best boned and rolled for slow or pot-roasting.

18 **Hanger/onglet** – barrel-shaped muscle adjacent to the diaphragm. Good for flash frying and long braising.

1   **Cheek** – for slow cooking.

6   **Bowler/Jewish fillet/round blade/ bullet muscle** – small fillet from the top rib. For slow cooking.

2   **Neck and clod** – rich flavour and best for stews, casseroles and braising, or for mince.

4   **Featherblade/flatiron** – tender, rich and well-marbled. Sear quickly or cook long and slow.

3   **Chuck and blade** – for casseroles, braising, pot-roasting and mince.

8   **Short-ribs/Jacob's Ladder** – for braising, or excellent for burgers if taken off the bone and minced.

21 **Brisket** – from the lower shoulder. Pot-roast or braise; use in pies and for smoking. Great for long and slow barbecuing.

22 **Shin** – rich meat for casseroles and slow-cooking.

Hindquarter

11 **Striploin** – roast on or off the bone, or cut into steaks for grilling or frying.

9   **Wing rib** – roast on the bone or boned and rolled.

12 **Sirloin/rump** – great as steak. Roast quickly at high heat and serve pink or slowly at a low temperature – both are good.

11 **T-bone/porterhouse** – striploin steak on one side and fillet on the other. Grill or fry.

10a/b Fillet

10a **Chateaubriand** – part of the fillet; used in Beef Wellington, roasts or steaks.

10b **Filet mignon** – lower, narrower end of the fillet. Slice into small steaks.

5   **Côte de Boeuf** – French name for trimmed single fore rib, also known as cowboy steak.

14 **Topside** – a lean cut with a layer of fat on top. Used for roasting or pot-roasting; can be diced for stewing too.

15b **Silverside** – lower part of the rump. Used for pot-roasts, braises, casseroles and salt beef.

15b **Salmon/eye of the round/ continental cut** – roast quickly at high heat and serve pink or dice for stewing.

16 **Top rump/knuckle** – for braises, casseroles, pies and stir-frying.

13 **Oxtail** – rich, unctuous flavour, for braises and casseroles.

17 **Shin** – for casseroles and stews.

19 **Flank** – a flat sheet with a coarse texture. Either cook long and slow or marinate, flash fry and slice into ribbons for serving.

20 **Skirt/bavette** – the thicker part of the flank, slow cook in stews and casseroles or marinate, flash fry and slice into ribbons.

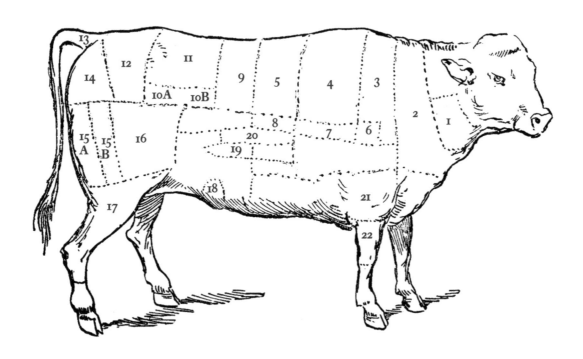

Fat

The Thorny Question of Fat

or: *Forget what you think you know – <u>why it is simply not true that all saturated fat is bad for you</u>.*

Until about thirty years ago, fat was at the centre of human diets and cultures around the world. Then a group of scientists determined that there was a link between saturated fat and heart disease, and the anti-fat movement was born. Jennifer McLagan has written on this subject in her book, *Fat: An Appreciation of a Misunderstood Ingredient*. She says that not only is our fat phobia overwrought, it also has not benefited our health in any way. Instead it has driven us into the arms of trans fats and refined carbohydrates, and fostered punitive, dreary attitudes toward food – that wellspring of life and pleasure. What we need to do is develop a healthy relationship with animal fats, which are fundamental to the flavour of our food.

Here are some facts about fat that may come as a surprise.

- Grass-fed cattle are ruminants that convert cellulose – which is literally indigestible for humans – into high-quality fat and protein.

- Grass-fed beef is as lean as a skinless chicken breast.

- Grass-fed beef has more omega 3 fats, vitamin A and E and the antioxidants lutein, zeaxanthin and beta-carotene than grain-fed beef. Traditionally reared beef also contains alpha lipoic acid, an antioxidant essential for cell metabolism, which lowers blood sugar and improves sensitivity to insulin.

- Grass-fed beef has the right ratio of omega 3 to omega 6 fats, i.e. about 1:1.

- Omega 3 fats help prevent obesity, diabetes and heart disease.

- The brain relies on omega 3 fats to fight depression, and to absorb the fat-soluble vitamins A, D, E and K.

- Polyunsaturated omega 6 fat, CLA, is almost unique to the fat of ruminants raised on grass; it is found almost exclusively in beef fat and butter. CLA is an exceptional omega 6 fat because it tends to act like an omega 3 fat, reducing triglyceride and the incidence of atherosclerosis. It also aids weight loss, reduces body fat and increases lean muscle, apparently by its effect on lipase, the enzyme used to digest fat.

- CLA is an antioxidant 200 times more powerful than beta-carotene. It helps to prevent cancer, and can slow the growth of tumours of the skin, breast, prostate and colon.

- From the Stone Age until relatively recently, fat was the measure of good eating. Traditional, natural fats are good for us; it is the new-fangled fats and trans-fats created in laboratories of which we should be suspicious.

- All fats are a mix of saturated, monounsaturated and polyunsaturated. A fat is described by its predominant fatty acid.

- Saturated fats are the most stable when heated; polyunsaturated fats are damaged by heating and become rancid and carcinogenic.

- Beef fat chips are better for you than chips made with polyunsaturated vegetable oils. Chips made with beef fat also taste better.

- Beef fat is typically 50–55% saturated and about 40% monounsaturated oleic acid, the same fatty acid found in olive oil, which lowers LDL (bad cholesterol) and keeps HDL (good cholesterol) level. Much of the saturated fat is stearic acid, which also lowers LDL.

- Saturated fats are powerful immune system boosters.

- Fat is tasty; it's what gives beef much of its flavour.

- Marrow is the oldest and simplest dish ever, prized even ahead of red meat by Stone Age hunters.

- The long-chain polyunsaturated fats in bone marrow helped grow the brains of early humans and distinguish them from apes.

Fats: the Basics

- All the traditional fats are healthy.

- The industrial diet contains too many omega 6 fats and too few omega 3 fats. This leads to obesity, diabetes, heart disease, cancer and depression.

- Trans-fats lower HDL (good cholesterol) and cause heart disease, among other ills.

- With animal fats, the animal's diet matters for our health.

- With vegetable oils, the processing matters for our health.

- Rather than being artery-clogging, saturated fats are vital to good health.

- Their most basic function is to make up half of cell membranes.

- They are required for the absorption of calcium and other minerals, and help the body retain the long-chain polyunsaturated fats such as the omega 3s in fish.

- Saturated fats fight harmful microbes, viruses and other pathogens.

What about Heart Disease?

- Saturated fats lower levels of lipoprotein (a), a substance that is implicated in clotting and atherosclerosis.

- Only 26% of the fatty plaques that cause heart attacks are made up of saturated fat.

- Half of blood cholesterol has nothing to do with diet. When you eat too much saturated fat, the body converts it into monounsaturated fat, which lowers LDL and leaves HDL alone. Stearic acid, the saturated fat in beef, actually lowers LDL cholesterol.

- Research by Dr Diana Schwarzbein shows that people with type 2 diabetes got worse on a low-fat/high-carb diet. She added a little fat and protein to her patients' diet and results were excellent: patients lost weight and had more energy. Blood sugar and cholesterol fell. Patients who 'cheated' by eating saturated fats and real mayonnaise, real eggs, real cheese and steak every day had the best results.

- A diet that includes plenty of fresh meat, fruit, vegetables, olive oil, fish, dark chocolate, walnuts and wine, and no trans-fats, refined vegetable oils, sugar or white flour is the healthiest for your heart.

(Adapted from *Real Food: What to Eat and Why* by Nina Planck.)

The Kit

The recipes in this book require very little specialist equipment. That said, cooking with good quality implements and equipment is far more enjoyable than it is when you use inferior versions. It would be worth investing in the following pieces of equipment:

- heavy, cast-iron, ridged griddle pan

- robust, heavy-duty roasting tin

- large, heavy, cast-iron casserole dish with a lid – as a brand, Le Creuset is hard to beat

- good-quality oven gloves

- kitchen tongs

- a couple of good, sharp knives – the Victorinox brand is less expensive than many others. Your butcher should be able to supply you with good professional knives at a reasonable price.

- a digital meat thermometer – we don't know what we'd do without one of these; it takes all the guesswork and stress out of the Sunday roast

- an oven thermometer – because ovens are not always accurate and temperatures do make a difference, particularly when roasting.

BEEF

IS THE

SOUL

OF

COOKING.

MARIE-ANTOINE CARÊME

Introduction

The recipes in this book are intended for the domestic cook. None of them is unduly challenging, and they are all achievable with very little in the way of fancy equipment. We have deliberately set out to keep the recipes simple, and the results delicious. We like big, gutsy flavours and we prefer a casual, family-style of presentation. There are no cheffy tricks here!

Most of the dishes are very forgiving, and we would encourage you to make substitutions and changes according to your taste. In some cases, though, precision is required – particularly when it comes to grilling or roasting meat. It's important to keep an eye on the time when you are using these methods.

We have made a point of encouraging the use of local ingredients where possible. We are lucky to have such wonderful ingredients to work with in Ireland – our produce is world class – and we will all benefit if consumers make a positive effort to buy Irish whenever possible.

We ate very well during the course of preparing the book and we hope that you will have as much pleasure trying the recipes as we did testing them.

Chapter 1
Steaks

Great steak is one of life's true pleasures, yet we are often disappointed when we order it in a restaurant or cook it at home. Sometimes, of course, that's down to the quality of the meat. You are much more likely to end up with a delicious steak when you start with grass-fed beef that's been dry-aged and handled properly at every step along the way. But the cooking method has a lot to do with maximising flavour too.

Steak Cooking Tips

- For fillet, striploin, T-bone, rib-eye and sirloin steaks – the classic cuts – buy steaks that are reasonably thick: 2–3cm at least.

- Remove the steak from the fridge an hour or two before you plan to cook it so that it starts out at room temperature. The thicker the steak, the longer it takes to come to room temperature.

- Use a cast-iron, ridged griddle pan.

- Heat it until it is smoking hot, so hot that you can barely hold your hand above it.

- Rub the steak with a little extra virgin olive or Irish rapeseed oil. Do not oil the griddle.

- Just before putting the steak on the pan, season it with flaky sea salt and plenty of freshly ground black pepper. The salt promotes what's known as the Maillard reaction – the browning and caramelising of the surface that makes steak taste so good.

- Once the steak is on the pan, don't move it around. This also helps with browning and caramelising. Turn it only once.

- Use the timings on pages 36–37. Err on the side of under-cooking rather than over-cooking – you can always put the steak back on the pan if it is too rare for your taste, but if it's overdone you can't uncook it.

- Leave the steak to rest – for at least 7 minutes. This improves texture and juiciness.

Steak Cuts

Sirloin steak

New York strip on the bone

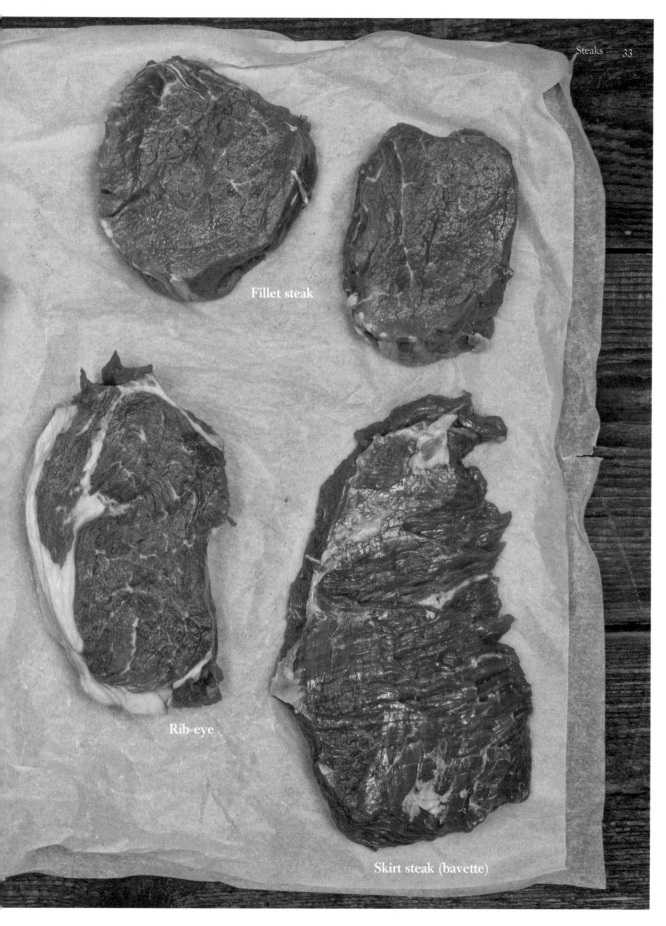

Fillet steak

Rib-eye

Skirt steak (bavette)

Hanger/onglet

Côte de Boeuf
(cowboy steak)

T-bone

Featherblade

Striploin

Steak Cooking Guide

All guidelines are for medium rare steak unless otherwise stated. Cooking times will vary according to the thickness of the steak, the heat of the pan and the temperature of the steak at the start of the cooking process.

Rib-eye

Rib-eye has become very fashionable over the past few years; you'll find it on a lot of restaurant menus where formerly you might have seen fillet or striploin. It comes from the fore-rib and has a band of fat running through it. This is what makes it so tasty; the fat bastes the steak from within as it cooks.

GUIDELINE: 4 MINUTES PER SIDE FOR MEDIUM RARE.

Featherblade/Flatiron

A small steak that comes from the shoulder blade, featherblade is not very well known. It's flavoursome, but should only be cooked rare if grilled – any more and it will be tough. Alternatively, it works well braised slowly, as in the recipe for Braised Featherblade with Parsley and Horseradish Dumplings on page 142.

GUIDELINE: 2¹/₂–3 MINUTES PER SIDE FOR RARE.

Côte de Boeuf/Cowboy Steak

This is a single rib beef chop, and will vary considerably in size depending on the animal it came from. Delicious and succulent.

GUIDELINE: SEAR FOR 5 MINUTES EACH SIDE. THEN PUT IT INTO A LOW OVEN (100°C/FAN 80°C/ GAS MARK ¹/₄) FOR ABOUT 35 MINUTES. USE A MEAT THERMOMETER TO CHECK THE INTERNAL TEMPERATURE – FOLLOW THE TABLE ON PAGE 63.

T-bone/Porterhouse

The T-bone comes from the lower middle of the animal. With fillet on one side and striploin on the other, it's impossible to get the cooking time completely right as each cut cooks differently.

GUIDELINE: A THICK T-BONE WILL TAKE 6 MINUTES PER SIDE. ALLOW 4 MINUTES PER SIDE FOR A THINNER ONE.

Striploin

If properly aged, striploin (which is called sirloin in the UK) is a flavoursome steak that has plenty of marbling. The cut comes from the middle back of the animal.

GUIDELINE: 3 MINUTES PER SIDE.

Fillet

Traditionally the most expensive cut of steak, the fillet comes from the inside of the sirloin. As it is a muscle that does no work, it is very lean and tender. Best served with a sauce on the side.

GUIDELINE: 3 MINUTES ON ONE SIDE AND 2 MINUTES ON THE OTHER.

Sirloin

From the hindquarter of the animal, sirloin steak (called rump steak in the UK) is full of flavour and good value. Buy it thick and cook it quick.

GUIDELINE: 3 MINUTES PER SIDE.

Skirt

Also known as bavette or flank, this is a distinctive, flat pleated cut of steak from the inner flank at the base of the diaphragm. Good flavour and great value. Benefits from marinating, depending on the recipe. Flank steak is from the thinner part of the same cut.

GUIDELINE: 2–3 MINUTES PER SIDE, LONGER IF CUT FROM THE THICKER END. SLICE AGAINST THE GRAIN.

Hanger

From the centre of the animal, this textured steak (known as onglet in France) is similar in shape to the fillet and runs next to the diaphragm. It has a distinctive, strong, almost kidney-like flavour. Ask your butcher to cut into the steak and remove the central sinew, which will leave two steaks about 20–30cm long.

GUIDELINE: COOK NO MORE THAN MEDIUM RARE, ABOUT 6 MINUTES ON ONE SIDE AND 4 MINUTES ON THE OTHER, DEPENDING ON THICKNESS. BEST SLICED AGAINST THE GRAIN.

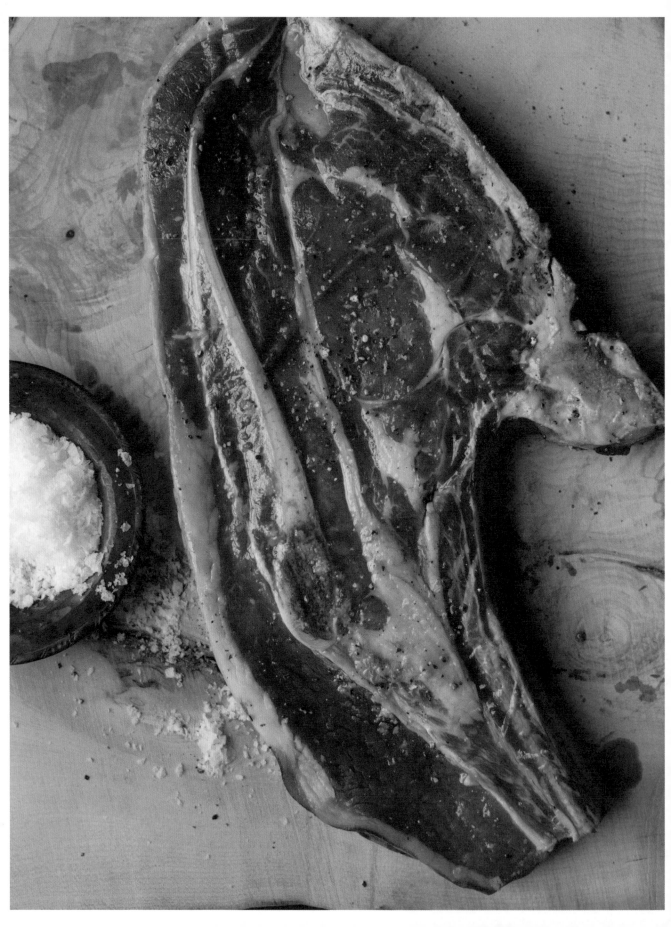

Good Things to Eat with Steak
Triple-Cooked Chips

Serves 1

You can make chips in a saucepan, but a domestic deep fat fryer is not very expensive and makes the whole process much safer.

200 g Maris Piper potatoes
dripping (enough to half-fill your pan when melted) or groundnut oil

Peel the potatoes and cut into chips: 1 cm thick for chunky chips; half that for skinny chips. Rinse well under cold water, then drain.

Put the chips into a pan of cold salted water and bring to the boil. Turn down the heat and simmer until the chips are just soft to the point of a knife.

Drain, pat dry, spread out on a flat tray and allow to cool; then put in the fridge until cold.

Heat the fat to 120° C and add the chips. Don't overcrowd the pan. Blanch for about five minutes until cooked through but not coloured.

Remove, drain, pat dry, spread out on kitchen paper on a flat tray, cool and refrigerate.

When you are ready to eat, heat the fat to 160° C and add the chips. Cook until crisp and golden, then remove, drain, season and serve immediately.

Oven Chips with Rosemary Salt

Serves 4

3 sprigs fresh rosemary
zest of 1 lemon
85 g sea salt
900 g Maris Piper potatoes, unpeeled, cut
  into large chips 1cm thick

100 ml extra virgin olive oil or Irish rapeseed
  oil
1 bulb garlic, cloves separated but unpeeled
freshly ground black pepper

Preheat the oven to 230° C/fan 210° C/gas mark 8. Place a baking tray in the oven.

To make the rosemary salt, remove the leaves from the rosemary, chop them and put in a mortar and pestle with the lemon zest and salt. Work to make a paste, adding more salt if the mixture is too wet. Spread out on a plate in a warm place to dry out a little.

Parboil the chips for about 10 minutes in boiling salted water.

Heat the oil in a frying pan, smash the garlic cloves under the flat side of a knife blade and add to the pan, followed by the chips. Toss in the oil until well coated, then season with pepper.

Bake on the preheated oven tray for 15–20 minutes until crisp and golden.

Sprinkle the rosemary salt on the chips before serving.

Grilled Mushrooms

Serves 4

8 large field mushrooms
30 ml extra virgin olive oil or Irish rapeseed oil
flaky sea salt
freshly ground black pepper

Put the mushrooms, gill side up, on a baking tray and drizzle with the oil. Sprinkle with plenty of sea salt and pepper.

Preheat the grill to low, and put the tray under the grill, not too close to the heat, until the mushrooms are cooked through. They should be very dark and moist.

Creamed Spinach

Serves 4

about 1 kg fresh spinach, washed and tough
  stems removed
2 tablespoons unsalted butter
100 g finely chopped shallots
1 teaspoon minced garlic

120 ml double cream
¾ teaspoon salt
½ teaspoon freshly ground black pepper
¼ teaspoon nutmeg

Bring a pot of salted water to a boil over high heat. Add the spinach and cook for 2 minutes. Drain in a fine mesh strainer, pressing with a large spoon to release as much water as possible. Finely chop and set aside.

Melt the butter in a frying pan over medium-high heat. Add the shallots and garlic and cook, stirring, until soft – about 2 minutes.

Add the spinach and cook, stirring, just until its liquid is released. Add the cream, salt, pepper, and nutmeg, and cook until the cream is reduced by half, about 4 minutes. Remove from the heat and serve immediately.

Roast Onions with Balsamic Vinegar

Serves 4–6

8 red onions, peeled and halved
100 ml extra virgin olive oil or Irish
  rapeseed oil
3 tablespoons balsamic vinegar

12 sprigs thyme
flaky sea salt
freshly ground black pepper

Preheat the oven to 190° C/fan 170° C/gas mark 5. Put the onions in a heatproof gratin dish or a small roasting tin in which they will fit snugly in a single layer.

Drizzle over the oil and balsamic and add the thyme and some seasoning. Make sure the onions are well oiled and seasoned.

Cook for 40 to 45 minutes, until tender and well browned.

Sauces to Serve with Steak
Salsa Verde

Serves 6

3 tablespoons roughly chopped flat-leaf
  parsley
1 tablespoon roughly chopped mint leaves
3 tablespoons capers
6 anchovy fillets
1 garlic clove, finely chopped

1 teaspoon Dijon mustard
juice of ½ lemon
120 ml extra virgin olive oil or Irish
  rapeseed oil
pinch of flaky sea salt

Blend together all the ingredients in a food processor or with a pestle and mortar until you have a thick paste. Taste and adjust salt and lemon as necessary.

Anchovy Butter

Serves 8

6 anchovy fillets, finey chopped
1 tablespoon flat-leaf parsley, finely chopped
2 tablespoons lemon juice
170 g unsalted butter, at room temperature

Blend the ingredients together, place on a sheet of clingfilm and roll into a sausage shape. Refrigerate until hard. Slice into discs as required.

Chimichurri

Serves 6

2 medium shallots, very finely chopped
1 clove garlic, very finely chopped
150 ml extra virgin olive oil or Irish
    rapeseed oil
large bunch flat-leaf parsley
    (leaves and stalks), finely chopped

leaves from a small bunch oregano
1 red chilli, seeded and finely chopped
a pinch of flaky sea salt
2 tablespoons freshly squeezed lemon juice

Combine the ingredients and let the mixture sit for an hour or so. Taste and adjust salt and lemon accordingly.

Béarnaise Sauce

This simplified, blender version of the classic recipe is Lucas Hollweg's.

3 sprigs tarragon
300 g butter
1 bay leaf
2 small shallots, thinly sliced
4 egg yolks

1 tablespoon white wine vinegar
a squeeze of lemon juice
a pinch of cayenne pepper
freshly ground black pepper
fine sea salt

Fill a blender with hot water to warm it.

Take the leaves from the tarragon sprigs and put the stalks in a small saucepan with the butter, bay leaf and shallots. Heat gently until the butter has melted.

Empty the water from the blender and dry it. Put the yolks and vinegar in the blender and blend for 30 seconds.

Reheat the butter until hot and bubbling. Switch on the blender and, with the motor running, strain the butter onto the egg yolks in a slow, thin stream, leaving the bay leaf, tarragon stalks and shallots in the sieve. The sauce will thicken to a thin, mayonnaise-like consistency.

Add a squeeze of lemon juice to taste, plus a tablespoon of just boiled water, and blend again.

Chop the tarragon leaves and add to the sauce, along with a pinch of cayenne, some freshly ground black pepper and a good pinch of salt. The sauce will hold for 20 minutes in a bowl suspended over a pan of hot water (off the heat) or for a few hours in a Thermos flask.

Romesco Sauce

Authentically, this is made with dried Spanish nora peppers, but they can be hard to find in Ireland. The sweet paprika is an acceptable substitute.

Serves 4

4 large ripe tomatoes
4 tablespoons extra virgin olive oil or Irish
  rapeseed oil
40 g whole blanched almonds
40 g hazelnuts
1 slice white bread

1 teaspoon sweet Spanish paprika
2 garlic cloves, crushed
1 tablespoon sherry vinegar
sea salt
freshly ground black pepper

Roast the tomatoes in a dry frying pan until the skins are blackened and the flesh cooked. Remove the skins and place the tomatoes in a food processor or blender.

Heat the olive oil in a frying pan over a medium to high heat and add the almonds, hazelnuts and bread. When golden brown, remove from the heat and leave to cool. Add to the tomatoes, along with the paprika, garlic cloves, sherry vinegar, sea salt and freshly ground black pepper and blend until combined but not too smooth – the sauce is better with a bit of texture. Taste and adjust the seasoning.

Mustard Sauce

Serves 8

300 ml single cream
300 ml Dijon mustard
80g flat-leaf parsley, finely chopped

Put the cream in a heavy-based saucepan, bring to the boil and let it boil for a few minutes until it has reduced by half. Whisk in the mustard, then remove from the heat and add the parsley.

Sirloin Steak with Red Wine Sauce

Serves 1

100 ml red wine
30 ml extra virgin olive or Irish rapeseed oil
4 sprigs thyme
3 cloves garlic, smashed

300 g piece sirloin steak
freshly ground black pepper
flaky sea salt

Combine the red wine, oil, thyme and garlic and pour over the steak. Marinate in the fridge, covered with clingfilm, for a couple of hours.

Season well with black pepper and sea salt flakes. Place on a very hot cast iron ridged pan (so hot that you can barely hold your hand near it) and cook for three minutes each side for medium rare.

Remove the steak and set aside to rest for at least five minutes.

Meanwhile, reduce the heat, add the marinade liquid and let it bubble for a minute or two. Serve with mashed potatoes and green vegetables, with the sauce poured over the steak.

Skirt Steak with Field Mushrooms and Truffle Oil

Serves 4

800 g skirt steak
flaky sea salt and freshly ground black
  pepper
120 g rocket leaves
extra virgin olive oil

600 g field mushrooms, sliced
2 garlic cloves, finely chopped
handful flat leaf parsley, chopped
1 tablespoon truffle oil

Heat a griddle pan to smoking. Rub the steak with a little oil, season it and cook for no more than 8 minutes in total (depending on thickness), turning half way through. Cover with foil and leave to rest in a warm place.

Make a salad with the rocket, dressed simply with a little olive oil, salt and freshly ground black pepper.

In a frying pan, fry the mushrooms with the garlic and most of the parsley in the olive oil until tender.

Slice the meat against the grain and arrange the slices on the rocket, with the mushrooms and the rest of the parsley scattered over the top. Drizzle with a little truffle oil.

Skirt Steak with Anchovies, Red Wine and Garlic

This is a great, gutsy marinade for skirt steak, which is called bavette in France. Be sure not to overcook the meat as this will make it tough: this cut should be served rare or medium rare.

Serves 4

leaves from 5 sprigs rosemary
1 large bulb garlic, cloves separated and
   peeled
2 tablespoons extra virgin olive or Irish
   rapeseed oil
100 g anchovies, drained

1 tablespoon Dijon mustard
375 ml red wine
freshly ground black pepper
zest and juice of a lemon
1 kg skirt steak
flaky sea salt

Very finely chop the rosemary leaves and garlic together.

Heat the oil in a frying pan and add the anchovy fillets. As they start to disintegrate, add the rosemary and garlic and fry for a minute or two, stirring. Do not let the garlic colour.

Stir in the mustard, wine, pepper and lemon zest and juice. Simmer until reduced by half.

Turn off the heat and allow to cool.

Cut the steak into two large pieces and put in a flat dish. Pour the marinade over, turning the steak a couple of times. Cover and marinate for between 2 and 4 hours – no longer – turning the meat a couple of times.

Heat a ridged griddle pan until smoking, season the steak with sea salt flakes and cook the skirt steak for about 2½–3 minutes on each side for medium rare, depending on thickness. Leave to rest for at least 7 minutes before serving.

Slice the meat across the grain and serve with crusty bread, a green salad and Dijon mustard.

Tagliata

This is Domini Kemp's version and very good it is too. You can make this with fillet, sirloin, striploin or rib-eye.

Serves 4

600–800 g fillet of beef (or sirloin, striploin or rib-eye)
salt and pepper
4 good handfuls rocket
8 Portobello mushrooms, peeled and cut into thick slices
Parmesan shavings

For the marinade:
100 ml balsamic vinegar
good few sprigs rosemary
8 cloves garlic, peeled
200 ml olive oil

Start by making the marinade. First remove all the leaves from the rosemary – you want a good tablespoon of rosemary leaves, even two. In a blender, whizz all the ingredients together. Season the marinade, which should be dark and thick. Pour it on top of the beef and leave for a while to marinate – a few hours would be great, or even overnight.

When you are ready to cook, put the rocket on each plate, along with some Parmesan shavings. Heat up a frying pan or griddle pan until it is really hot. And if your pan is a regular size, you may need to do this in two batches.

Let the excess marinade run off the beef and then sear and brown it at a very high temperature. Use the guide on p. 36 to guage the time. Turn the steaks over when they release themselves; and when you have great colour on them, set them aside to rest.

Finish cooking any remaining steaks if necessary, otherwise fry the chunky mushrooms and pour any remaining marinade on top. They don't need much cooking; they will absorb the marinade. Heat up thoroughly till they get slightly charred and burnt at the edges and are piping hot. At this stage, you can slice the beef and arrange beef slices and mushrooms on top of the rocket and serve straight away.

Chapter 2
Roasts

The key to successful roasting is using the right method for the cut that you have. Use the wrong method, and you'll end up with something that's as tough as shoe leather. Use the right method, and even the lowliest cut of beef will be transported to the heights of deliciousness. It's all about doing justice to the cut and treating it correctly.

Roast Cuts

Rib-eye

Rib on the bone

Housekeeper's cut

Brisket

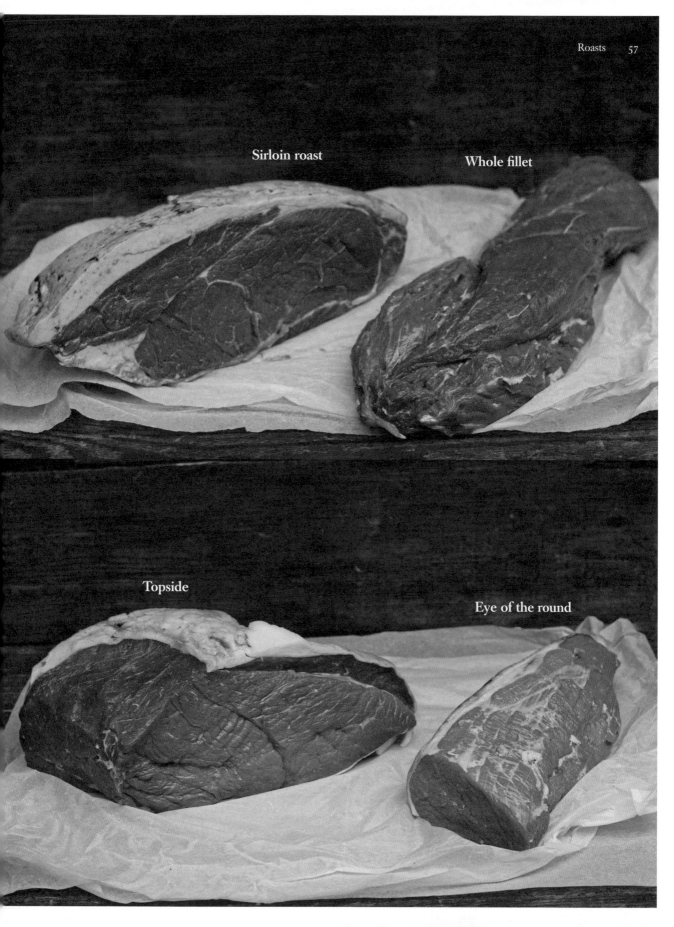

Sirloin roast

Whole fillet

Topside

Eye of the round

Brisket on the bone

Silverside

Oven-roasting Tips

- Make a timetable, working back from when you plan to sit down and incorporating time for both cooking and resting the meat.

- It sounds obvious, but don't attempt to make more elements of a roast dinner than you have oven space for. If you have one oven, you can roast meat and potatoes, and make Yorkshire puddings while the meat is resting, but you may not be able to do roasted vegetables as well.

- Always remove the meat from the fridge a couple of hours before you plan to cook it; cooking times will be more accurate if the meat starts out at room temperature.

- Choose a robust tin that will be able to sit on the hob without buckling when you're making gravy.

- Use a roasting tin that's not too big for the piece of meat that you're cooking. If the tin is too big, the juices released during roasting will spread out over the surface area of the tin and burn. You want to contain them so that they are not wasted and will contribute to a flavoursome gravy.

- Cook in the middle of the oven if possible – that's where the temperature is most accurate and consistent.

- Season the meat just before you pop it into the oven. Modest salting with flaky sea salt helps create the crust and the flavours associated with browning (the Maillard reaction); too much salt and the meat will dry out. Plenty of freshly ground black pepper is good.

- If you are roasting a lean cut such as topside or silverside, ask your butcher to tie on a piece of suet for extra lubrication. This is known as barding.

- Use a meat thermometer. It will make your life so much easier, and take the guesswork out of knowing when the meat is cooked how you like it.

Rib on the Bone: the Roast of Roasts

There are few reactions as satisfying for the cook as the one you get when you bring a majestic rib roast of beef to the table. The smells emanating from the kitchen are beyond seductive, and the appearance of the meat does not disappoint. We'd always suggest buying a piece bigger than you think you need, because the leftovers will make for a few happy lunches the next day and will disappear before you know it.

Other cuts that are good to roast on the bone are sirloin from the hindquarter and wing rib.

Serves 10

4–6 kg rib of beef
extra virgin olive oil, Irish rapeseed oil or soft dripping
fine sea salt and freshly ground black pepper

Preheat the oven to 230° C/fan 210° C/gas mark 8.

Rub the joint all over with the oil or soft dripping and season with salt and pepper. Place the meat in a heavy-duty roasting tin and cook for 30 minutes, until browned and sizzling.

Turn the heat down to 160° C/fan 140° C/gas mark 3 and open the oven door for a minute to accelerate the drop in temperature.

Give the joint a further 9–10 minutes per 500 g for very rare meat, 12–15 for medium or 18–20 if you prefer it well done. As all ovens vary, a meat thermometer is invaluable, as it will give you the confidence to know the exact moment when the beef is cooked to your liking. (See the chart on page 63.)

Remove the meat from the oven and place on a warm platter in a warm place, covered loosely with foil. Leave it to rest for at least half an hour before carving – this allows the meat to relax and improves its flavour and juiciness.

Gravy

Pour the juices and fat that have accumulated in the roasting tin into a Pyrex jug. The fat (dripping) will rise to the top and you can spoon most of this off and reserve it.

Return the residue to the roasting tin and place on top of a low heat. If you want a thicker gravy, add a teaspoon or two of flour now, scattered across the tin. Gradually add half a bottle of red wine and 500 ml of beef stock, stirring as you do so to ensure that the flour is absorbed.

Simmer for fifteen minutes or so, scraping the tin to ensure that no flavour is lost, until the gravy has thickened slightly. Taste and adjust the seasoning, sieve and serve.

Guideline Roasting Times

WEIGHT UNDER 2KG:

- 20 minutes at 230° C/fan 210° C/gas mark 8.
- Then reduce oven temperature to 160° C/fan 140° C/gas mark 3 and continue to cook at the lower temperature:
    - for rare beef – 10 minutes per 500 g
    - for medium beef – 15 minutes per 500 g
    - for well-done beef – 20 minutes per 500 g

WEIGHT 2–5KG:

- 30 minutes at 230° C/fan 210° C/gas mark 8.
- Then reduce oven temperature to 160° C/fan 140° C/gas mark 3 and continue to cook at the lower temperature:
    - for rare beef – 10 minutes per 500 g
    - for medium beef – 14 minutes per 500 g
    - for well-done beef – 19 minutes per 500 g

WEIGHT OVER 5KG:

- 40 mins at 230° C/fan 210° C/gas mark 8.
- Then reduce oven temperature to 160° C/fan 140° C/gas mark 3 and continue to cook at the lower temperature:
    - for rare beef – 9 minutes per 500 g
    - for medium beef – 12 minutes per 500 g
    - for well-done beef – 18 minutes per 500 g

Use a meat thermometer to ensure accuracy and reduce stress! This is particularly helpful when you are cooking larger roasting joints: the shape of the piece of meat, the temperature of the oven and the temperature of the meat when it started cooking will all affect the total cooking time. The internal temperatures to aim for are:

- very rare – 45° C
- rare – 50° C
- medium rare – 55° C
- medium – 60° C
- medium to well done – 65° C
- well done – 70° C

This is the reading at the point the meat comes out of the oven; the temperature will rise by a few degrees as the meat rests.

Foolproof Rib-eye Roast

Serves 6

1.5 kg rib-eye roast
extra virgin olive oil or Irish rapeseed oil or soft dripping
flaky sea salt and freshly ground black pepper

This is an example of the timing for one specific roast:

The meat went into the oven for 20 minutes at 230° C/fan 210° C/gas mark 8, then the temperature was reduced and the meat roasted for a further 15 minutes per 500 g at 160° C/fan 140° C/gas mark 3. The meat was taken out at an internal temperature of 55° C and rested for 20 minutes, and it was perfectly medium rare. Total cooking time: 1 hour 5 minutes.

Other boneless cuts suitable for roasting in this way: rib rolled, sirloin rolled.

Ultra Slow-Roast Sirloin

Very slow roasting is the answer when you have to go out and want dinner to be ready when you come home. This method produces a very juicy and flavoursome roast.

Serves 4–6

1.5 kg sirloin
1 tablespoon extra virgin olive or Irish rapeseed oil
flaky sea salt and freshly ground black pepper

Preheat the oven to 75° C/fan 55° C/gas mark ¼.

Rub the sirloin with the oil and season with flaky sea salt and freshly ground black pepper. Place a ridged griddle pan over a high heat and when it's smoking, sear the meat on all sides until well browned.

Place the meat in a roasting tin and cook for 4–5 hours, or until a meat thermometer reads 50° C (for rare meat), 55° C (medium rare) or 60° C (medium). Start checking the temperature after four hours.

Cover with foil and leave to rest for 30 minutes before serving. This would be excellent with Béarnaise sauce (see page 45).

The Trimmings
Individual Yorkshire Puddings

Everyone loves Yorkshire pudding – fact. A muffin tin is ideal for making these attractive individual puddings, but you can of course use the mixture to make one large pudding that you serve in slices – it's your choice. Either is delicious.

Serves 6 greedy people (makes 12 muffin-sized puddings)

150 g plain flour
6 eggs
150 ml milk
110 ml water
sea salt and freshly ground black pepper
beef dripping, melted (to grease the tin)

Sift the flour into a bowl and make a well in the centre. Add the eggs and incorporate gradually, using an electric hand whisk. Add the milk, water and seasoning and whisk until the batter is smooth.

When the beef is ready to come out of the oven, increase the heat to 220° C. Use a pastry brush to grease the muffin tin (or a roasting tin) with the melted dripping and place it in the oven to heat.

After about ten minutes, add the batter to the tin and return to the oven on as high a shelf as you can for about 25–30 minutes, or until the puddings have risen and look crisp and golden. While the puddings are cooking, get everything else ready. Serve immediately.

Beef Dripping Roast Potatoes

Allow 2–3 floury potatoes per person. Peel the potatoes and cut into roughly equal pieces. The more surface area there is, the more opportunity you have to create a crunchy exterior.

Par boil the potatoes in a large saucepan of salted water for about 7 minutes, or until there starts to be a little 'give' on the surface when scraped with the tines of a fork.

Drain and return to the saucepan, put the lid on and give it a good shake to roughen the potatoes' surfaces a little.

Put a few tablespoons of dripping (or goose fat, Irish rapeseed oil or extra virgin olive oil if you prefer) into a roasting tin and place in the oven with the meat for about 10 minutes. Add the potatoes to the tin, turning to ensure that they are basted in the fat. Sprinkle with fine sea salt.

Cook for about an hour or until crisp and golden. You can leave them in after the meat comes out of the oven and turn up the heat if you think they need it.

Horseradish Mash

Allow a couple of floury potatoes per person. Boil the potatoes in salted water in their skins until tender.

Meanwhile, heat some whole milk and butter (allow approximately 250 ml whole milk and 125 g butter per kg of potatoes) in a saucepan, add a couple of tablespoons of freshly grated horseradish and leave to infuse.

Drain the potatoes in a colander and leave until cool enough to handle. Peel the potatoes and break them up roughly with a fork to allow more steam to escape. Reheat the milk, butter and horseradish mixture and use a potato ricer to add the potatoes into the hot liquid. Whisk until smooth and season with fine sea salt and freshly ground black pepper to taste.

On the Side: Sauces
Creamed Horseradish

Serves 8–10

100 g horseradish root, peeled and grated
2 tablespoons white wine vinegar
1 teaspoon English mustard
a pinch of sugar

100 g crème fraîche
3 tablespoons cream
a pinch of fine sea salt
freshly ground black pepper

Combine the horseradish with the vinegar, mustard and sugar. Leave for 10 minutes. Stir in the crème fraîche and cream and season to taste with salt and pepper.

Horseradish and Dijon Mustard Yoghurt Crème Fraîche

Serves 8–10

100 g horseradish root, peeled and grated
1 tablespoon Dijon mustard
60 g natural yoghurt

60 g crème fraîche
a pinch of fine sea salt
freshly ground black pepper

Combine the horseradish, mustard, yoghurt and crème fraîche. Leave for 10 minutes. Taste and season with salt and pepper.

Wild Garlic Aïoli

Serves 6–8

2 organic egg yolks
1 teaspoon Dijon mustard
125 ml extra virgin olive or Irish rapeseed oil
125 ml sunflower oil

juice of ½ lemon
2–3 tablespoons minced wild garlic
fine sea salt to taste

Whisk the egg yolks in a medium bowl until pale yellow, about 3–5 minutes. Add the mustard, and whisk for another minute. Add the oil, very slowly, just a few drops at a time, whisking all the time. Gradually add the lemon juice, then the wild garlic and sea salt.

Roast Fillet with Wild Garlic Salsa Verde

Serves 6

Wild garlic is one of the harbingers of spring. Forage for it yourself or take the easy way out and buy some at your local farmers' market or from a speciality food store. Of course, the season is short, so you could use a classic salsa verde recipe (page 44) instead. Serve the fillet warm or at room temperature – the meat will be tender and the flavour better.

1.2 kg beef fillet, trimmed
1 tablespoon extra virgin olive oil or Irish rapeseed oil
flaky sea salt and freshly ground black pepper

FOR THE WILD GARLIC SALSA VERDE:
80 g wild garlic, finely chopped
80 g fresh basil, finely chopped
4–5 anchovy fillets, finely minced
1 heaped tablespoon capers, finely minced
1 heaped teaspoon Dijon mustard
juice of ½ large or 1 small lemon
125 ml extra virgin olive oil or Irish rapeseed oil
flaky sea salt and pepper to taste

Preheat the oven to 220° C/fan 200° C/gas mark 7.

Make the salsa verde by combining all the ingredients in a bowl and leave to stand for at least an hour. Taste and adjust the seasoning.

Place a heavy frying pan over a high heat until smoking. Rub the meat with the oil and season well with plenty of salt and a few twists of freshly ground black pepper. Sear the meat on all sides until it has a crisp, brown crust.

Place the meat in a roasting tin and put in the oven. Cook for 12–15 minutes, no longer. Check the internal temperature against the chart on page 63. Remove from the oven, cover with foil and leave to rest in a warm place for at least 20 minutes.

Serve in thick slices with the salsa verde.

Roast Fillet with Prosciutto

An impressive dish for a buffet table, this is simple to make and can be prepared ahead of time. Serve at room temperature.

Serves 10

1.5 kg beef fillet, cut from the middle
1 tablespoon extra virgin olive oil or Irish
  rapeseed oil
flaky sea salt
freshly ground black pepper
20 slices prosciutto
3–4 tablespoons Dijon mustard

Preheat the oven to 200° C/fan 180° C/gas mark 6.

Heat a heavy frying pan until smoking. Rub the fillet with the rapeseed oil and season generously with sea salt and freshly ground black pepper. Sear the meat until browned on all sides. Allow to cool slightly.

Lay the prosciutto out on greaseproof paper in overlapping rows so that it makes a rectangular shape. Coat the beef all over with mustard and place it on the prosciutto. Wrap the prosciutto around the beef and secure with string.

Sit the fillet on a roasting tray and roast for 30 minutes for rare, 40 minutes (medium) or 50 minutes (well done). Check the internal temperature against the chart on page 63 to ensure that the beef is cooked to your liking.

Leave the beef to cool in the roasting tray. Dab with kitchen paper to remove any excess juices.

Carve into thin slices and serve on a platter, or serve whole and allow people to help themselves.

Topside with a Dill and Mustard Dressing

Rare roast topside is a cut that works as well cold as it does hot. Think of vitello tonnato and it will give you a good idea of how the meat will be when sliced very thinly and served at room temperature. Slow roasting is the key to retaining juiciness and a pink centre. Topside cooked this way is excellent for sandwiches and salads.

Serves 8

2 kg topside, in one piece
2 tablespoons extra virgin olive oil or Irish
   rapeseed oil
sea salt and freshly ground black pepper

FOR THE DILL AND MUSTARD DRESSING:
4 tablespoons Dijon mustard
1½ tablespoons red wine vinegar
2 teaspoons caster sugar
175 ml extra virgin olive oil or Irish rapeseed
   oil
1 tablespoon hot water
leaves from a small bunch of dill, chopped

Preheat the oven to 220° C/ fan 200° C/gas mark 7.

Rub the meat with the oil and season all over with salt and black pepper. Place in the oven for 30 minutes, then turn down the heat and cook at 150° C/fan 130° C/gas mark 2 for 10 minutes per 500 g, or until the internal temperature is about 55° C, at which point it will be perfectly medium rare.

To make the dressing, whisk together the mustard, vinegar and sugar. Add the oil slowly, drop by drop at first and then in a thin stream, whisking all the time, until the sauce is thick. Loosen with the hot water and stir in the chopped dill.

Remove the meat from the oven, cover with foil and allow to cool to room temperature. Serve with the dill mustard dressing, or with a simple dressing of olive oil, lemon juice, chopped flat-leaf parsley and capers.

Alternatively, rest the meat for 20 minutes and serve with all the trimmings (see pages 66-68).

The Eye of the Round: Beef or Salmon?

A few years back there was a champion racehorse called Beef or Salmon, said to have been named after the inevitable, unchanging main course choices offered to guests at functions held in Dublin's Burlington Hotel.

The shape of the whole eye of the round cut gives it its alternative name – 'salmon' of beef. We were sceptical about the merits of roasting this cut for a short time at a high heat, but we gave this recipe from the Ginger Pig a try and were converted. The key is leaving the meat to relax for a good 15 minutes, which tenderises it well. There's still a fair chew to this cut, but the flavour is great and it will appeal to fat-phobes as it is very lean. The centre will be a pale, rosy pink rather than a rare red at an internal temperature of 50° C.

Serves 4–5

2 tablespoons tamari or soy sauce
1 teaspoon English mustard
1.1 kg eye of the round
sea salt
freshly ground black pepper
1 tablespoon extra virgin olive oil or Irish
   rapeseed oil

Preheat the oven to 220° C/fan 200° C/gas mark 7.

Mix the tamari or soy sauce with the English mustard and rub over the meat. Season all over with the salt and black pepper.

Heat the oil in a solid roasting tin. Add the meat to the tin and roast for about 35–40 minutes, until a meat thermometer gives a reading of about 50° C. Remove from the oven and allow to rest in a warm place, covered with foil, for at least 15 minutes before carving. Serve with mustard and horseradish sauce.

Traditional Pot Roast of Housekeeper's Cut with Winter Vegetables

This is a forgiving pot roast that takes very little time to prepare and scant attention while it's cooking. It is a hearty and economical family meal that will be much appreciated on a miserable winter evening. You can play around with the vegetables and use a combination of swede, celeriac and butternut squash if you prefer.

Serves 6–8

1 tablespoon extra virgin olive oil or Irish rapeseed oil
2 kg housekeeper's cut
4 small whole onions or shallots, peeled
500 g carrots, peeled and cut into large chunks
500 g parsnips, peeled and cut into large chunks
2 heads of garlic
a few sprigs each of fresh parsley and thyme
250 ml beef or chicken stock
sea salt and pepper

Preheat the oven to 150° C/fan 130° C/gas mark 2.

Heat the oil in a heavy casserole dish and brown the meat on all sides. Add the vegetables, garlic, herbs and stock. Season and cover with foil and a tight-fitting lid.

Place in the oven and cook for 2½–3 hours or until tender. Slice the meat and serve with the vegetables and cooking juices.

An accompaniment of champ, colcannon or the horseradish mash on page 68 would be delicious.

Brisket and Butternut Squash Pot Roast with a Rosemary Gremolata

Serves 4–6

You could use topside, silverside or housekeeper's cut for this hearty winter pot roast, but brisket probably has the best flavour.

2 tablespoons extra virgin olive oil or Irish rapeseed oil
1.2 kg brisket, boned and rolled
fine sea salt
freshly ground black pepper
1 onion, peeled and chopped
2 parsnips, peeled and quartered
2 carrots, peeled and halved
½ butternut squash, peeled and cubed
400 g Jerusalem artichokes, peeled and halved

500 g small potatoes
1 handful fresh sage leaves
2 tablespoons tomato purée
½ bottle red wine
350 ml beef or chicken stock

FOR THE GREMOLATA:
zest of 1 lemon, grated
the leaves from a handful of rosemary, finely chopped
2 cloves garlic, finely chopped

Preheat the oven to 150° C/fan 130° C/gas mark 2.

Heat the oil in a large ovenproof casserole dish, season the brisket with fine sea salt and freshly ground black pepper and sear until it is brown all over. Remove the meat and set it to one side.

Add the onions, parsnips, carrots, butternut squash, Jerusalem artichokes, potatoes and sage to the pot and cook for a few minutes, stirring, until the vegetables are lightly browned.

Add the tomato purée, wine and stock and stir. Return the brisket to the pot and bring to a simmer. Season. Cover with tin foil and a tight-fitting lid and place in the oven for about 3 hours or until the meat is tender.

Meanwhile, combine the ingredients for the gremolata.

Remove the meat from the sauce and skim off any excess fat. Slice the meat and serve in bowls with the vegetables, topped with gremolata.

Chapter 3
The Classics

These are the most famous beef dishes in the world for good reason, and they are a terrific way to showcase quality meat. We love experimenting with new ideas and picking up on food trends as much as the next person, but sometimes there is nothing better than a classic dish executed perfectly.

Steak Tartare

Some people use fillet, others striploin. Sirloin works too. The meat you use must be of excellent quality; you have to have absolute trust in your butcher. It's important to hand-chop the meat with your sharpest knife, and taste the mixture as you go along, tweaking until you have the balance just right. We prefer the raw egg mixed in rather than perched on top. Even if you think you couldn't bring yourself to eat raw meat, you really should try this once. You might just be converted.

Serves 4

2 organic egg yolks
2 tablespoons Dijon mustard
4 anchovy filets, finely chopped
2 teaspoons tomato ketchup
1 teaspoon Worcestershire sauce
Tabasco sauce, to taste
freshly ground black pepper
50 ml extra virgin olive oil or Irish
  rapeseed oil

30 ml brandy
1 small shallot, finely chopped
50 g capers, rinsed
50 g cornichons, finely chopped
2 tablespoons flat-leaf parsley, finely chopped
500 g striploin steak, finely chopped
4 slices good white bread, toasted and
  quartered

Place the egg yolks in a large stainless steel bowl and add the mustard and anchovies. Mix well, then add the ketchup, Worcestershire sauce, Tabasco and pepper, and mix well again.

Slowly whisk in the oil, then add the brandy and mix again. Fold in the shallot, capers, cornichons and parsley. Add the chopped meat to the bowl and mix well.

Divide the meat evenly among four chilled dinner plates, forming it into a disc on each plate. You can use a ring mould if you have one, but it's not essential.

Serve with the toasted bread. Skinny chips (see the recipe on page 39) are the classic accompaniment.

Spiced Beef

We have been making spiced beef at James Whelan Butchers ever since the first shop opened in the 1960s. It is a tradition at Christmas, and the smell of spiced beef cooking is as evocative as mulled wine and mince pies when it comes to festive ambience. Spiced beef works well in summer salads too. Your pharmacist should be able to help you source the saltpetre.

Serves 10

2.5–3 kg eye of the round, topside or
    silverside of beef
75 g brown sugar
25 g black peppercorns
12 g allspice berries

25 g juniper berries
12 g ground cloves
12 g sea salt
12 g saltpetre

Trim the beef, then rub it all over with the sugar. Leave it in a bowl in the fridge for two days. Crush the peppercorns, allspice and juniper berries together in a pestle and mortar. Mix with the cloves, salt and saltpetre.

Rub the beef thoroughly with the spices. Cover and keep in the fridge for 6–7 days. Turn the beef in the mixture daily.

Preheat the oven to 140° C/fan 120° C/gas mark 1.

Place the beef in a deep casserole dish as near to its size as possible. Add 250 ml water and cover tightly.

Cook the beef in the oven for 5 hours. Leave it to cool in the liquid for 2–3 hours, then remove and wrap it in tin foil. Store in the fridge.

Beef Wellington

There's something wonderfully retro about the notion of beef Wellington. It puts us in mind of formal dinners at Downton Abbey or seventies dinner parties with the hostess floating around in a kaftan. Named after the man who crushed Napoleon at Waterloo, the very notion of preparing beef Wellington casts fear into the hearts of the most competent of home cooks. Perhaps that's why so many chefs like to cook it at home for their private celebrations, in a subtle display of one-upmanship. You'll find more chefs eating beef Wellington than turkey on Christmas Day, that's for sure. But we'll wager that even they don't make their own puff pastry. Our version doesn't include foie gras (it just seems de trop) and it isn't that difficult. Really.

Serves 6

20 g dried porcini mushrooms
100 g butter
4 shallots, finely chopped
600 g chestnut mushrooms, chopped
leaves from 2 sprigs of thyme
400 ml Madeira
4 tablespoons double cream

2 tablespoons extra virgin olive oil or Irish
  rapeseed oil
1 kg centre-cut beef fillet
500 g all-butter puff pastry
1 egg, beaten

Preheat the oven, and a baking sheet, to 200° C/fan 180° C/gas mark 6.

Soak the porcini in 150 ml boiling water for 20 minutes, then squeeze out and chop finely, reserving the soaking water.

Melt the butter in a frying pan over medium heat and cook the shallots until pale gold, then add the mushrooms, porcini and thyme and cook until softened. Pour in the Madeira, season, turn up the heat and cook until the wine has evaporated.

Take off the heat and scoop the mixture into a bowl. Mix in the double cream, taste for seasoning, and set aside. This is your mushroom duxelle.

Heat the oil in a pan over a high heat and, when it is smoking, add the fillet and sear briefly on all sides until crusted. Season well and allow to cool.

Roll out the pastry to a rectangle big enough to envelop the meat. Brush the pastry all over with most of the beaten egg, and then spread with the duxelle mixture.

Put the beef at one end and carefully roll it up in the pastry. Stand the pastry-enveloped beef seam side down, and then trim the edges and tuck in to seal the parcel, pressing the edges together. Brush with the remainder of the beaten egg.

Put on to the hot baking sheet and cook for about 35–40 minutes, or until a meat thermometer reads 45° C for very rare or 60° C for medium and the pastry is golden. Set aside to rest for 5 minutes before serving.

Boeuf Bourguignon

The great Elizabeth David brought joy through food to depressed post-war Britain – in her own way, she was quite the revolutionary. In *French Provincial Cooking*, which was first published in 1960 and has never been out of print, she describes boeuf à la Bourguignonne (to give it its full title) as one of the 'carefully composed, slowly cooked dishes which are the domain of French housewives and owner-cooks of modest restaurants, rather than of professional chefs ... Such dishes do not, of course, have a rigid formula, each cook interpreting it to [their own] taste.' This is our version, but feel free to play around with it and make it your own.

As with all slow-cooked beef dishes, it will be even better on the second day. Allow it to cool before refrigerating it overnight and reheat it the next day.

Serves 4–6

a few tablespoons plain flour	300 g button mushrooms
sea salt	2 medium onions, chopped small
freshly ground black pepper	200 g streaky bacon, cut into short strips
1 kg chuck or shin beef, in large pieces	4 cloves garlic, peeled and lightly crushed
about 2 tablespoons extra virgin olive oil or	2 bay leaves
Irish rapeseed oil	1 large sprig of thyme
knob of butter	1 bottle red wine
around 20 shallots or small onions, peeled	200 ml stock

Put a few tablespoons of flour in a bowl and season generously with sea salt and black pepper. Toss the meat in the seasoned flour.

Put a couple of tablespoons of oil and a knob of butter in a heavy casserole dish over a medium heat. Add the pieces of meat in batches, leaving plenty of space between the pieces. Don't move the meat around much; just turn it occasionally until it is all browned on all sides. Browning the meat is key to the flavour of the final dish, so it's important that the meat is not crowded – if it is, it will steam rather than brown. Add a little more oil and butter as necessary.

As each batch of meat browns, remove and place to one side. When all the meat is browned, add the shallots to the casserole and brown lightly, then add the mushrooms and cook until golden. Remove the shallots and mushrooms and set to one side.

Add the chopped onion and streaky bacon to the casserole and cook until the onions are soft and the bacon lightly golden.

Return the beef to the pan with the garlic, bay leaves, thyme, wine and stock. Season. Simmer, uncovered, over a low heat for at least an hour and a half, then return the shallots and the mushrooms to the casserole and cook for another 30 minutes.

Steak Diane

Steak Diane, named after the Greek goddess of the hunt, is one of those 1950s classics that makes you think of movie stars and dressing for dinner. Associated with 21 and The Colony in New York, its popularity waned – along with that of crêpes Suzette and baked Alaska – as rising rents required restaurateurs to put tables closer together and thus put paid to potentially risky flambéing at the table. It's definitely worthy of a special occasion.

Serves 2

2 x 175 g fillet or striploin steaks
sea salt and freshly ground black pepper
25 g unsalted butter
1 shallot, finely chopped
55 g button mushrooms
25 ml brandy
125 ml double cream

½ teaspoon Dijon mustard
1 teaspoon Worcestershire sauce
1 tablespoon finely chopped flat-leaf parsley

Flatten the steaks with a rolling pin or meat hammer until about 1.5–2cm thick. Season well. Melt half the butter in a frying pan over a medium heat until it foams. Add the steaks and fry for 2 minutes on each side for medium rare. Remove the steaks, cover with foil and leave to rest in a warm place.

Add the remaining butter to the pan, add the shallot and fry until soft. Add the mushrooms and cook for a couple of minutes, until they start to soften.

Add the brandy, light it carefully with a match and allow the flames to subside. Add the cream, mustard, Worcestershire sauce and reduce for a couple of minutes – you're looking for the consistency of single cream. Stir in the parsley and check the seasoning.

Serve the steak with the sauce on top and skinny chips (see the recipe on page 39) on the side.

Beef Stroganoff

Traditionally, beef Stroganoff is made with fillet steak, but we think that sirloin has more flavour and is better value. The dish is named after the Russian Stroganov family, whose private chef created the dish for them. It's another one of those retro classics that, if made well, is universally popular.

Serves 4

500 g sirloin steak
1 teaspoon hot paprika
2 teaspoons sweet paprika
sea salt
freshly ground black pepper
100 g butter
1 tablespoon extra virgin olive oil or Irish
    rapeseed oil

2 medium onions, sliced
350 g chestnut or flat mushrooms, sliced
1 tablespoon Dijon mustard
75 ml white wine
125 ml crème fraîche
juice of ½ a lemon (optional)

Cut the beef into strips about 5 cm by 0.5 cm wide. Mix together the paprika, salt and pepper and coat the meat with the mixture.

Heat half the butter with the oil in a shallow pan, add the onions and cook until soft but not browned. Add the mushrooms and cook until tender.

In another pan, heat the remaining butter. When it sizzles, add the beef and cook over a high heat until starting to brown – you want the meat to be still pink inside. This will only take a minute or two.

Add the mustard to the onion and mushroom mixture, then add the white wine and boil to reduce by half.

Stir in the crème fraîche, bring back to the boil and season. Add some lemon juice if you like the sauce a little sharper. Turn the heat down and add the beef and its juices.

Serve with wide flat noodles.

Beef Carpaccio with Desmond Cheese

A simple and very elegant dish. Excellent dry-aged fillet of beef served in this way is a real pleasure. Be sure to use very good olive oil – you will really notice the difference. Many hard cheeses will work here – and Parmesan or pecorino would be authentic – but if you are feeling patriotic, experiment with an Irish cheese.

Serves 4

400 g beef fillet
6 tablespoons extra virgin olive oil, plus extra
  for drizzling
2 tablespoons lemon juice

flaky sea salt
freshly ground black pepper
1 bulb fennel, finely sliced
50 g Desmond cheese, finely shaved

Either ask your butcher to oblige, or cut the beef into very thin slices against the grain and place between the sheets of clingfilm. If you have a meat tenderiser, beat the meat gently until you have very thin slivers. Alternatively, use the pressure of a rolling pin to make the slices as thin as possible. Arrange the slices on a large platter.

Combine the olive oil, lemon juice, sea salt and black pepper and drizzle over the meat. Leave to one side for five minutes to allow the dressing to flavour the meat.

Scatter the fennel slices across the meat, and top with the shavings of cheese. Drizzle with some more olive oil.

Beef Goulash

Rib-sticking stuff for a winter's day; there's nothing better after a bracing country walk. And the fact that it's a one-pot wonder only makes it more attractive.

Serves 6

3 tablespoons extra virgin olive oil or Irish rapeseed oil
2 onions, peeled and diced
2 cloves garlic, peeled and minced
½ teaspoon caraway seeds
1 kg beef shin, cut into 3 cm cubes
1½ tablespoons sweet paprika
¼ teaspoon cayenne pepper
1 bay leaf
2 green peppers, cored, deseeded and cut into thin strips
1 x 400 g tin chopped tomatoes
2 medium-sized potatoes, peeled and cut into 3 cm cubes
sea salt and freshly ground black pepper
150 ml sour cream
bunch of chives, chopped

Heat the oil in a large heavy saucepan over a medium-low heat and fry the onions until they are soft and translucent, about 15 minutes. Add the garlic and caraway seeds, fry for a further minute, then scrape the onion mixture into a bowl.

Raise the heat, add the rest of the oil and brown the meat, in batches, on all sides. Remove from the heat and return the onions to the pan along with the paprika and cayenne. Stir until the meat is well coated with onions and spices.

Add the bay leaf and just enough water to cover the meat by about 3cm. Bring to the boil, then reduce the heat and simmer gently, uncovered, for about an hour, or until the meat is tender.

Add the peppers, tomatoes and potatoes. Season and simmer for a further 20 minutes. Serve with a dollop of sour cream and sprinkled with chives.

Daube with Macaroni
St Gall Gratin

As with beef Bourguignon, there are as many variations on the theme of daube as there are cooks in Provence. You can cook a daube with chunks of meat – shin would be good – or in the piece, pot-roast style. Here we have used the so-called housekeeper's cut, which is taken from the shoulder of the animal and is ideally suited to a long, slow braise in the oven while you get on with something else. The gratin is delicious.

Serves 6

1.5 kg housekeeper's cut, rolled and tied
1 tablespoon plain flour
2 tablespoons extra virgin olive oil or Irish
  rapeseed oil
1 x 400 g tin chopped tomatoes
500 ml beef or chicken stock
250 g macaroni
150 g St Gall cheese, grated

FOR THE MARINADE:
1 bottle red wine
100 ml brandy
2 tablespoons extra virgin olive oil or Irish
  rapeseed oil

2 tablespoons red wine vinegar
3 onions, halved and sliced
2 carrots, sliced
1 stick celery, sliced
4 cloves garlic, sliced
2 bay leaves
1 orange, juice and zest, in strips
6 black peppercorns
6 allspice berries
2 cinnamon sticks
2 sprigs fresh thyme
1 teaspoon fine sea salt

Put the beef in a large bowl with all the marinade ingredients. Leave to marinate overnight. Preheat the oven to 140° C/fan 120° C/gas mark 1.

Lift the marinated meat from the bowl and pat dry with kitchen paper. Dust it thoroughly with the flour.

Heat the oil in a casserole and brown the meat all over, turning it a couple of times. Add the tomatoes and stock and stir well.

Add the marinade with the vegetables. Bring to a simmer, cover and transfer to the oven. Cook slowly for about three hours, after which it will be beautifully tender.

Remove the meat from the cooking liquid, cover it with foil and keep warm. Strain the liquid, skim the fat from the surface and boil to reduce by half.

Meanwhile, cook the macaroni until just short of al dente. Add the macaroni and half the cheese to the cooking liquid and season with salt and pepper. Sprinkle the remaining cheese on top, turn the oven up to 180° C/fan 160° C/gas mark 4 and reheat for 10–15 minutes. Heat under the grill for a few minutes to brown the top of the gratin. Slice the meat and serve with the macaroni, making sure that everyone gets some of the crisp topping.

Corned Beef with Parsley Sauce

It's easy to forget how wonderful corned beef can be. This is a favourite recipe that makes a very popular family dinner. It's worth making extra for sandwiches or corned beef hash the next day.

Serves 4 (with leftovers)

1 kg silverside corned beef
2 carrots, chopped
1 onion, chopped
2 tablespoons butter
2 tablespoons plain flour
200 ml milk

2 tablespoons finely chopped fresh parsley
1 teaspoon English mustard
pinch of nutmeg
salt and pepper

Put the corned beef, carrots, and all but one tablespoon of the chopped onion into a large pot, cover with water, and bring to a boil over high heat.

Reduce to a simmer and skim off the foam that accumulates on the surface of the water.

Cover and simmer for about 2½ hours, or until the corned beef is tender. Remove from the liquid, wrap in foil, and set aside. Reserve about 200ml of the cooking liquid.

Melt the butter in a small saucepan over medium heat. Mince the reserved onion and add to the butter. Cook for about 1 minute, then stir in the flour and cook, stirring, for about 1 minute more. Add the reserved cooking liquid, milk, parsley, mustard, nutmeg, and salt and pepper to taste, whisking the ingredients together until smooth. Cook for another 4–5 minutes, whisking constantly, until the sauce thickens.

To serve, slice the corned beef against the grain and spoon the sauce over it.

Delicious with buttered cabbage and floury boiled potatoes or colcannon.

Corned Beef Hash

This is the ultimate hangover breakfast, and very good even if you haven't over-indulged the night before.

Serves 2

2 tablespoons Worcestershire sauce
1 tablespoon wholegrain mustard
200 g corned beef, cut into 1 cm cubes
275 g waxy potatoes, unpeeled and chopped
   into 1 cm cubes
4 tablespoons extra virgin olive oil or Irish
   rapeseed oil

1 large onion, quartered and thinly sliced
sea salt
freshly ground black pepper
2 eggs

Combine the Worcestershire sauce and mustard in a cup and pour over the beef, mixing it around to distribute it evenly.

Simmer the potato cubes in boiling salted water, covered, for 5 minutes. Drain and cover with a tea towel to absorb the steam.

Heat the oil in a frying pan until very hot and fry the onion until very well browned. Remove the onions from the frying pan and keep to one side.

Add a little more oil to the pan and fry the potatoes until they too are well browned. Return the onions to the pan and season. Add the beef and keep everything in the pan moving until the beef is heated through. Turn the heat down.

In another frying pan, fry the two eggs in a little oil. Divide the hash between two plates and serve with an egg on top of each.

Tomato ketchup is essential.

Tournedos Rossini

It's hard to conceive of a dish more decadently luxurious than tournedos Rossini, a dish that is said to have been dreamed up by the 'king of chefs and chef of kings' Marie-Antoine Carême and the composer Gioachino Rossini in the kitchen of the House of Rothschild in Paris. Tournedos Rossini rarely appears on menus any more, but perhaps it is due a revival. In any case, it's a recipe worth having in your arsenal for when a truffle and some foie gras just happen to come your way. Or you win the lottery.

Serves 4

1 tablespoon olive oil
1 tablespoon butter
4 x 200 g fillet steaks
sea salt and freshly ground black pepper
4 x 50 g slices foie gras (optional)
1 tablespoon port

2 tablespoons brandy
2 tablespoons Madeira, plus a little extra
100 ml beef stock
2 garlic cloves, very finely sliced
1 truffle, thinly sliced
4 slices white bread

Add the oil and butter to a hot skillet or frying pan. Season the steaks. When the butter is foaming, add the steaks and cook over a high heat for 2–3 minutes on each side until the meat is nicely browned. Remove from the pan and leave to rest in a warm place, covered with foil.

Add the slices of foie gras to the hot pan, sear them very quickly, then remove from the pan and place on a sheet of kitchen paper.

Deglaze the pan with the port, brandy and 2 tablespoons of the Madeira. Add the stock and reduce the heat. Let the sauce bubble until it starts to thicken.

To a separate pan add a dash of Madeira and the garlic, then add the sliced truffle. Braise gently for a couple of minutes and then add the reduced sauce to the pan.

Toast the bread. Place each steak on a slice of toast, top with the foie gras and pour over the truffle sauce.

Chapter 4
Quick

These are the recipes for when you need something on the table in jig time. Some need a little marinating, or other advance preparation, so read the recipe through before starting to make sure that it's going to work for you in the time that you have available. Asian flavours work particularly well in this speedy kind of cooking, so you'll find that quite a few of the recipes have an Asian twist.

Skirt Steak with Green Herb Sauce

Fat-phobes love this cut of steak as no trimming is required. Don't skip the marinating stage, though – that's what keeps the meat juicy and tender.

Serves 4–6

a whole skirt steak
8 sprigs rosemary
8 cloves garlic, unpeeled and smashed
freshly ground black pepper
2 tablespoons extra virgin olive oil or Irish
   rapeseed oil
flaky sea salt

FOR THE HERB SAUCE:
2 cloves garlic, peeled and crushed
75 ml white wine vinegar
1 teaspoon ground cumin
1 teaspoon sea salt
4 (in total) large handfuls of mint, coriander
   and flat-leaf parsley leaves
250 ml extra virgin olive or Irish rapeseed oil
1 whole red chilli, deseeded and chopped
   finely

Put the steak in a bowl with the rosemary, garlic, plenty of freshly ground black pepper and the oil. Cover with clingfilm and leave to marinate for at least a couple of hours, preferably overnight, turning a couple of times if possible. Take the steak out of the fridge about an hour before you are ready to cook.

To make the herb sauce, blend together the garlic, vinegar, cumin and salt in a food processor. Add the herbs and blend to a purée. With the motor running, gradually add the oil until you have a loose sauce. Stir in the chopped chilli. You can make this ahead of time – just stir before serving.

Cut the steak into two large pieces. Heat a large, ridged cast iron pan – or two if you have them – on a high heat until you can barely hold your hand over it. Remove the steak from the marinade and season well with sea salt flakes.

Cook for 2–3 minutes each side, without moving the meat, depending on how you like your steak cooked. Two and a half minutes is bang on for medium rare if the skirt steak is thin; thicker steak will take longer so adjust accordingly. Take care not to overcook – you will end up with tough steak.

Remove from the pan and leave to rest for 5–10 minutes, covered with foil. Repeat with the second piece of meat (if you are only using one ridged pan).

Slice the meat across the grain and serve on a board, dressed with any juices that have run out during resting and a little of the sauce, with the rest of the sauce on the side.

This is very good with the red slaw and sweet potato wedges on page 187.

Skirt Steak Fajitas

Family-friendly midweek suppers don't get much tastier than this.

Serves 4

600 g skirt steak
2 tablespoons extra virgin olive or Irish
    rapeseed oil
2 cloves garlic, crushed
juice of 1 orange
1 red chilli, finely chopped

TO SERVE:
4 wraps
guacamole (see page 148)
salsa (see page 148)
100 ml crème fraîche
100 g Cheddar cheese (e.g. Hegarty's), grated

Marinate the steak in the oil, garlic, orange juice and red chilli for half an hour, while you make the guacamole and salsa.

Heat a ridged griddle pan to smoking hot and sear the steak for about 3 minutes on each side.

Leave to rest for 10 minutes before slicing across the grain and serving with the wraps (warmed), guacamole, salsa, crème fraîche and grated cheese.

Sweet potato wedges or rice on the side would be good.

Beetroot, Jerusalem Artichoke and Skirt Steak Salad with Toasted Hazelnuts and Mixed Leaves, Tarragon Dressing

If you have leftover rare roast beef, particularly topside (see the recipe on page 176), this is a lovely way to use it up, rather than cooking steak especially. Jerusalem artichokes are in season in the winter months, but if you can't find them, use celeriac or even roasted carrots instead. You can roast the beetroot and artichokes ahead of time.

Serves 4

600 g skirt steak
5 tablespoons extra virgin olive oil or Irish
  rapeseed oil
8 cloves garlic, smashed
8 stalks tarragon
8 medium-sized beetroots, scrubbed
3 tablespoons balsamic vinegar
flaky sea salt
500 g Jerusalem artichokes, peeled
freshly ground black pepper

150 g hazelnuts, toasted and the skins
  rubbed off
200 g mixed salad leaves

FOR THE DRESSING:
1 tablespoon Dijon mustard
2 tablespoons white wine vinegar
5 tablespoons extra virgin olive or Irish
  rapeseed oil
3 tablespoons finely chopped tarragon leaves

Preheat the oven to 200° C/fan 180° C/gas mark 7.

Mix 2 tablespoons of the oil with the garlic cloves and tarragon in a bowl. Add the steak, cover in clingfilm and leave to marinate in the fridge for a couple of hours.

Trim the beetroot, cut into quarters and toss with a couple of tablespoons of oil and the balsamic vinegar. Place in a roasting dish and sprinkle with flaky sea salt.

Cut the artichokes into chunks, toss with a tablespoon of oil and sprinkle with salt. Place in another roasting dish in the oven.

Keep an eye on the beetroots and artichokes while they are roasting: you want them to be tender and starting to caramelise, which will take about an hour.

Make the dressing by whisking together the mustard, white wine vinegar and oil. Add the chopped tarragon.

Season the steak with flaky sea salt and freshly ground black pepper and sear in a ridged griddle pan over a high heat for about 3 minutes on each side. Cover with foil and leave to rest for 10 minutes while you assemble the salad.

Combine the beetroot, Jerusalem artichokes, leaves and hazelnuts. Slice the steak against the grain and add to the salad. Add the dressing and toss.

Steak Sandwich

Hanger steak – also known as onglet – has a distinctive flavour that gives a run of the mill steak sandwich a delicious intensity. Ask your butcher to remove the sinew and prepare it for grilling.

200 g hanger steak per person
extra virgin olive or Irish rapeseed oil
flaky sea salt
black pepper
1 handful of rocket per person
¹/₃ baguette per person
horseradish mustard crème fraîche dressing
   (see recipe on page 69)

Rub the steak with oil, season well and sear on a very hot pan for 3 minutes on each side, which will bring it to medium rare.
   Leave to rest for 10 minutes while you make the dressing (see page 69).
   Slice the steak and serve in a good baguette with rocket and dressing.

Beef Larb with Lettuce Wraps

This is the national dish of Laos, but it appears in various incarnations throughout Southeast Asia. Often made with pork or chicken, it's equally good with beef. Play around with the proportions to get the balance of sharpness and heat that you like best. This is a super-speedy starter that's fun to eat, or a quick supper that you can have on the table in minutes.

Serves 6 as a starter, 2 as a main

1 teaspoon extra virgin olive oil or Irish rapeseed oil

2 red chillies, finely chopped (use bird's eye chillies if you can take the heat)

2 cloves garlic, finely chopped

400 g minced beef

1 tablespoon Thai fish sauce (nam pla)

4 spring onions, finely chopped

zest and juice of 1 lime

4 tablespoons coriander, finely chopped

2 heads of iceberg lettuce

TO GARNISH:
finely sliced shallots
100 g toasted peanuts, chopped

Put the oil in a frying pan on medium heat, add the finely chopped chillies and garlic and cook for a couple of minutes, stirring occasionally.

Add the beef, turn up the heat and cook for 3–4 minutes or until no trace of pink remains, breaking up the meat as it cooks. Add the fish sauce and cook until the liquid evaporates.

Off the heat, stir in the spring onions, the zest and juice of the lime and the coriander. Taste and add more lime juice if you like. Fill the iceberg lettuce leaves with scoops of the meat and serve with shallots and peanuts on the side. Eat with your fingers.

Beef Teriyaki with Spring Onions

This Japanese dish is very easy to make and, in our experience, universally popular! Marinate ahead for a very quick supper.

Serves 4

8 tablespoons soy sauce
4 tablespoons mirin
4 tablespoons caster sugar
1 tablespoon honey
1 tablespoon sesame oil
2 teaspoons finely grated ginger

1 garlic clove, thinly sliced
800 g piece sirloin steak
1 tablespoon extra virgin olive oil or Irish
   rapeseed oil
bunch of spring onions
sushi rice

Place the soy sauce, mirin, sugar, honey, sesame oil, ginger and garlic in a saucepan over medium-high heat. Bring to the boil, reduce the heat to low and simmer for 5–10 minutes. Remove from the heat and allow to cool to room temperature.

Pour the soy sauce mixture into a large, shallow dish and add the steak, turning a few times to coat. Cover and refrigerate for at least 3 hours.

Drain the beef, reserving the marinade. Heat the oil in a large frying pan over medium-high heat. Cook the steak for about 3 minutes each side (for medium rare) or according to how you like it. Transfer the steak to a plate, cover loosely with foil and leave to rest for 5 minutes. Cook the spring onions in the frying pan and set to one side.

Add the reserved marinade to the pan and bring to the boil. Reduce the heat to low and simmer, uncovered, for 2–3 minutes or until reduced slightly.

Thinly slice the steak. Serve with sushi rice, prepared according to the instructions on the packet, and sliced spring onions, drizzled with the sauce.

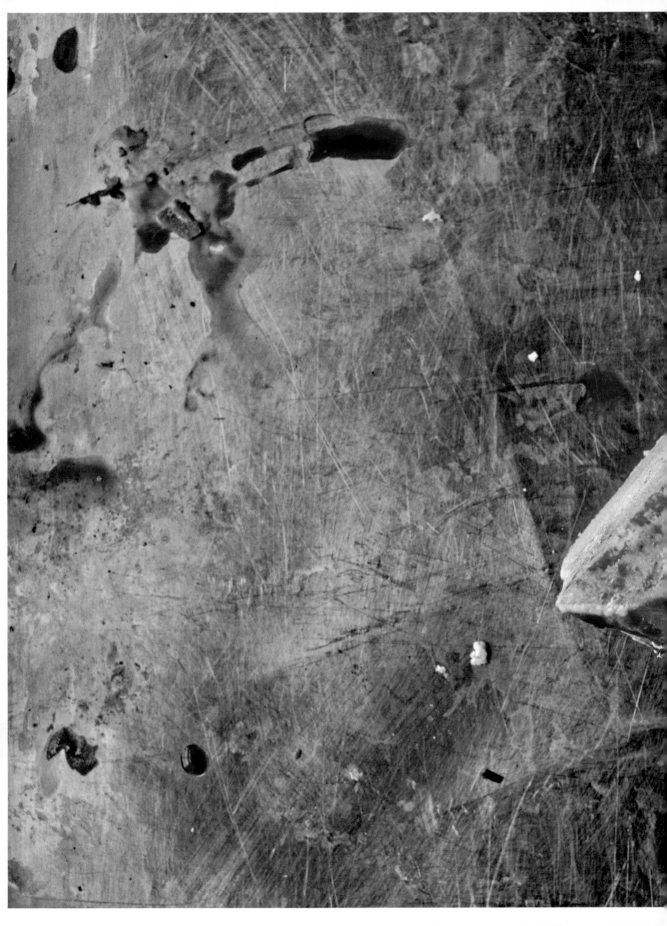

Beef Tataki

A truly fresh and vibrant salad that takes next to no time to prepare. This works well as either a starter or a main course.

Serves 6 as a starter

500 g beef fillet
30 ml extra virgin olive oil or Irish
    rapeseed oil
flaky sea salt
freshly ground black pepper

FOR THE MARINADE:
75 ml soy sauce
50 ml rice vinegar
2 shallots, finely sliced
2 tablespoons soft dark brown sugar
zest of 1 lime
10 g fresh ginger, grated
2 garlic cloves, sliced

FOR THE SALAD DRESSING:
50 ml soy sauce
50 ml rice vinegar
1 tablespoon soft dark brown sugar
1 lemon, juice and zest only
1 chilli, finely chopped

FOR THE SALAD:
a handful of beansprouts
a handful of watercress
½ cucumber, sliced
1 shallot, sliced
2 teaspoons pickled ginger

Rub the beef with oil and season with salt and freshly ground black pepper. Heat a heavy-based frying pan and fry the beef for one minute on each side. Remove from the pan and set aside. Mix together all the ingredients for the marinade in a bowl until well combined. Place the meat in the bowl and massage the marinade into it. Transfer the meat and marinade to a Ziploc bag and leave in the fridge to chill for at least two hours.

Make the dressing by whisking together all the ingredients in a bowl until well combined. Arrange the salad on a large platter and spoon over the dressing. When the meat has been chilled, slice it very thinly and arrange on top of the salad.

Pomegranate-Marinated Hanger Steak with a Warm Farro Salad

Ask your butcher to prepare the hanger steak for grilling; it will probably be in a few pieces once the sinew has been removed.

This recipe will work equally well with sirloin or skirt steak, but check the cooking guide on page 37 and adjust the timing accordingly.

Farro is a nutty-tasting whole grain from Italy; you could use brown basmati rice or a barley couscous instead.

Serves 4

2 tablespoons extra virgin olive oil or Irish rapeseed oil
2 tablespoons pomegranate molasses
1 tablespoon sherry vinegar
500 g hanger steak
200 g farro
1 large bunch flat-leaf parsley, chopped
1 pomegranate, seeds only
100 g walnuts, toasted
sea salt

FOR THE DRESSING:
1 clove garlic, crushed
1 tablespoon sherry vinegar
4 tablespoons extra virgin olive oil or Irish rapeseed oil
2 teaspoons sumac
pinch of ground coriander
pinch of ground allspice
pinch of freshly ground black pepper
pinch of sea salt

Mix the oil, pomegranate molasses and sherry vinegar in a bowl. Put the steak in a flat dish and cover with the marinade. Leave for an hour or two, turning a couple of times.

Meanwhile, simmer the farro in a litre of water for about 35 minutes or until tender. Make the dressing: combine the ingredients and check the seasoning.

When the farro has been simmering for about 15 minutes, heat a griddle pan until smoking, season the steak with sea salt and cook for about 3 minutes on each side, until nicely charred. This will bring the steak to medium rare/medium – cook it any longer and it will be tough. Cover with foil and leave to rest.

When the farro is tender, drain it and dress it while still warm. Add the pomegranate seeds, parsley and walnuts. Slice the steak in strips against the grain. Divide the farro salad between four plates and serve with the slices of steak on top.

Truffled Fillet of Beef and Hegarty's Cheddar Sandwich

This is one of the most stylish fast food dishes imaginable, and you can prepare it in the time it takes to order a takeaway. Perfect for a summer lunch in the garden with a bottle of lightly chilled red wine. Or inside if the weather doesn't oblige.

Serves 6

800 g fillet of beef, trimmed
2 tablespoons extra virgin olive oil or Irish
   rapeseed oil
flaky sea salt
coarsely ground black pepper

2 sourdough baguettes
90 g black truffle butter, at room temperature
60 g hard cheese, such as Hegarty's Cheddar
80 g rocket

Preheat the oven to its hottest setting.

Rub the beef with the oil and season well. Sear on a hot frying pan on all sides, then place in the oven and cook for 35 minutes or until a meat thermometer reads 45° C (for very rare), 50° C (rare), 55° C (medium rare) or 60° C (medium).

Remove the beef from the oven, cover it tightly with aluminium foil, and allow it to rest at room temperature for 15 minutes. Slice the fillet.

Cut the baguettes lengthwise but not all the way through. Spread the bottom halves generously with the truffle butter. Top with a layer of sliced beef and sprinkle with salt and pepper.

Top with shavings of cheddar and a sprinkling of rocket leaves. Fold the tops of the sandwiches over, cut each baguette diagonally into 3 sandwiches, and serve straight away.

Weeping Tiger Salad

Despite the name, this is not a fiercely hot salad, although you can add more and hotter chillies if that is your preference. You can also make it a more substantial meal by adding rice or egg noodles to the salad.

Serves 4

800 g sirloin steak
extra virgin olive oil or Irish rapeseed oil
flaky sea salt

FOR THE DRESSING:
2 shallots, finely chopped
6 tablespoons lime juice
4 tablespoons Thai fish sauce
4 tablespoons chopped fresh coriander
1 teaspoon caster sugar
1 finely chopped red chilli

FOR THE SALAD:
335 g beansprouts
2 carrots, peeled and sliced into ribbons
1 red chilli, finely chopped
1 cucumber, peeled and deseeded, cut into
  chunks
200 g mixed salad leaves
1 large bunch coriander, leaves only
2 tablespoons sesame oil
100 g chopped roasted cashews

Heat a cast iron griddle pan over a high heat until smoking. Lightly oil the steak on both sides and season with flaky sea salt. Sear for 3 minutes on each side. Leave to rest for 5 minutes.

Combine all the dressing ingredients together in a bowl and stir. In another bowl, combine the beansprouts, carrots, chilli, cucumber, salad and coriander leaves, and drizzle with the sesame oil. Mix well and add the dressing.

Arrange the salad on a platter and top with the roasted cashews. Slice the steak and arrange on top of the salad.

Beef and Green Vegetable Stir Fry with Oyster Sauce

Serves 4

600 g sirloin steak
sea salt
freshly ground black pepper
2 teaspoons coriander seeds
400 g green vegetables, e.g. tenderstem
  broccoli, asparagus, pak choi
2 tablespoons extra virgin olive oil or
  Irish rapeseed oil

1 red onion, peeled and finely sliced
2 cloves garlic, peeled and finely sliced
1 thumb-sized piece fresh ginger, peeled and
  finely chopped
3 tablespoons soy sauce
1 teaspoon sesame oil
3 tablespoons oyster sauce
red chilli, finely sliced, to serve (optional)

Slice the steak into strips and season with salt and pepper. Grind the coriander seeds in a pestle and mortar, and add to the seasoned steak.

Blanch the vegetables in boiling water for a minute and refresh under cold water so that they retain their vibrant colour.

Heat a wok until very hot. Pour in a tablespoon of oil and add the onion, garlic and ginger. Fry for a couple of minutes until the onion starts to soften. Add another tablespoon of oil and the beef and stir-fry for a couple of minutes. Add the vegetables and fry for a further 2 minutes, stirring all the time. Add the soy sauce, sesame oil and oyster sauce and stir until everything is well coated.

Serve with noodles or steamed jasmine rice. Scatter with finely sliced red chilli if you like a little more heat.

Skirt Steak with Caramelised Onions, Hamptons Style

Janet O'Brien is an Irishwoman who caters some of the smartest parties in the Hamptons, New York. She's far too discreet to name her clients; suffice to say they are both great and good, and run the gamut from politicians to film stars to rappers. This is her favourite beef recipe. The marinade is a great staple for the fridge as it lasts for weeks and can be used for chicken, pork and vegetables as well as beef. The quantities given here will make enough marinade to last a while.

Serves 2

2 pieces skirt steak, about 250 g each
flaky sea salt

FOR THE MARINADE:
120 ml extra virgin olive oil
120 ml soy sauce
120 ml Worcestershire sauce
3 cloves garlic
10 cm piece fresh ginger, finely grated

FOR THE CARAMELISED RED ONIONS:
30 g butter
2 tablespoons extra virgin olive oil
1 tablespoon balsamic vinegar
4 red onions, peeled, halved and sliced very
   thinly

Blend together all the ingredients for the marinade. Marinate the steak overnight.

Prepare the onions by heating the butter, oil and balsamic vinegar in a large frying pan. Add the onions and cook slowly, uncovered, until the onions are caramelised and the juices have almost completely evaporated. Put the onions to one side and keep warm.

Preheat the barbecue or heat a cast iron ridged griddle pan until very hot.

Season the steaks with flaky sea salt and cook for 2½ minutes each side for rare. Leave the steak to rest for 7 minutes. Slice very thinly against the grain and place on top of the warm caramelised red onions.

At the highest-end parties of the Hamptons, this is often served on a bed of rocket leaves that have been tossed in lemon juice and extra virgin olive oil, with a sprinkle of sea salt. The chimichurri recipe on page 45 would also go very nicely.

Beef Noodle Soup with Pak Choi

Speedy and very tasty, this is one of those dishes that makes you realise that cooking at home is so much better (and better for you) than ordering takeout.

Serves 2

4 tablespoons sake
3 tablespoons mirin
1 tablespoon soy sauce
3 cloves garlic, finely chopped
1 red chilli, finely chopped
300 g sirloin steak, cut into strips

1 tablespoon extra virgin olive oil or Irish
  rapeseed oil
500 ml beef or chicken stock
100 g rice vermicelli noodles
2 heads of pak choi
small bunch of fresh coriander, chopped

Combine the sake, mirin, soy sauce, garlic and chilli. Add the strips of beef and leave to marinate for an hour if you have time.

Heat the oil in a frying pan, remove the beef from the marinade with a slotted spoon and fry over a high heat for a couple of minutes, then add the marinade and fry for another minute.

Meanwhile, bring the stock to the boil in a saucepan, add the noodles, cook for a minute and then add the white parts of the pak choi and cook for another minute. Then add the beef and the green parts of the pak choi.

Deglaze the frying pan with a ladle of the stock, adding the dark liquid to the broth. Serve in deep bowls with the fresh coriander sprinkled on top.

Chapter 5
Long &
Slow

This is the chapter we hope you will turn to when you have a little time to spend pottering in the kitchen and experimenting with some of the wonderfully flavoursome cuts that benefit from gentle, slow cooking, either in the oven or on the hob. Many of the cuts used in the recipes in this chapter are interchangeable – ask your butcher about acceptable substitutions if you aren't sure.

Most of these recipes will taste even better if you cook them the day before you plan to eat, refrigerate overnight and reheat gently. There's a mysterious alchemy that happens when all the flavours have the time and opportunity to get to know each other. Most also freeze well, so it's worth making a double quantity and popping half in the freezer.

Slow Cuts

Short ribs

Bone-in shin
(osso bucco)

Chopped chuck

Cheeks

Multi-tasking Rich Beef Cheek Ragù

You could use this sauce with pasta, on top of a baked potato, in one of the pasta dishes in Chapter 7, with a soft cheesy polenta (see the next page) or simply with mashed potatoes and green vegetables. It is rich, unctuous and entirely wonderful. It also freezes beautifully, so if you get your hands on a quantity of beef cheeks, make a big batch, use some for supper and then sit back and gloat. Did someone say smug?

This quantity is enough for two lasagne recipes (see page 192).

Serves 8

1.8 kg beef cheeks, trimmed
sea salt
black pepper
2 tablespoons extra virgin olive oil or Irish rapeseed oil
120 g smoked bacon, chopped into cubes
4 carrots, chopped
4 onions, chopped

4 sticks celery, chopped
3 x 400 g tins chopped tomatoes
375 ml red wine
1 litre chicken stock
a few sprigs of thyme
2 tablespoons aged balsamic or saba vinegar, or vino cotto

Preheat the oven to 170°C/150°C fan/gas mark 3½.

Cut the beef cheeks in half and season with sea salt and black pepper. Heat a couple of tablespoons of oil in a heavy frying pan and fry the beef cheeks in batches, allowing them to brown and caramelise. Do not overcrowd the pan, or the meat will steam rather than brown.

Meanwhile, in a large, heavy-bottomed casserole dish, fry the bacon until golden, add the chopped vegetables and fry until softened. Add the tomatoes and then the beef cheeks.

Pour the red wine into the frying pan and scrape away any crispy bits, then add to the casserole dish. Add the chicken stock, cover and cook in the oven for about 3 hours, by which time the beef cheeks should be falling apart.

Remove the lid and cook for about a further 45 minutes, stirring occasionally, until some of the liquid has evaporated and you have a rich, thick sauce. Break up the meat with a wooden spoon. When the sauce has cooled slightly, add the balsamic or saba vinegar or vino cotto, which adds richness, and check the seasoning.

This will be even better if you allow it to cool, refrigerate it overnight and use it the following day.

Soft Polenta with Cheese

125 g quick-cook polenta
250 ml hot chicken stock
pinch chilli flakes
1 tablespoon finely chopped fresh rosemary
sea salt and freshly ground black pepper
60 g cheese, such as Desmond, Hegarty's,
    Coolea or Cratloe Hills (or Parmesan, of
    course), grated

Put the polenta and chicken stock in a saucepan over a medium heat. Add the chilli flakes, chopped rosemary, sea salt and black pepper and bring to the boil.

Reduce the heat and simmer for 2–3 minutes, or until all the stock has been absorbed and the polenta is no longer grainy. Stir in the cheese.

Beef with Anchovies and Olives

We've stolen this recipe from Diana Henry, a wonderful British food writer, and tweaked it slightly. Don't be put off by the anchovies, and certainly don't tell any self-professed anchovy haters what's responsible for the wonderfully intense umami flavours that this dish delivers in spades. Any of the slow-cooking cuts will work here; just keep an eye on the cooking time according to which cut you use.

Serves 6

4 tablespoons extra virgin olive oil or Irish rapeseed oil
1.2 kg braising beef, cut into chunks
1 large onion, roughly chopped
8 garlic cloves, chopped
2 fennel bulbs, trimmed and diced
8 anchovies
1 teaspoon ground cinnamon
1 bottle red wine
1 tablespoon tomato purée

2 strips orange zest
juice of 1 orange
2 rosemary sprigs
freshly ground black pepper
200 g wrinkly black olives

FOR THE GREMOLATA:
a handful of flat-leaf parsley
2 garlic cloves
finely grated zest of 1 unwaxed lemon

Preheat the oven to 170° C/fan 150° C/gas mark 3½.

Heat three tablespoons of oil in a heavy ovenproof casserole dish and brown the meat in batches. Don't overcrowd the pan – you want the meat to catch and caramelise as it cooks, rather than steam. This will add to the complexity of flavour of the finished dish. Remove the meat and set aside.

Add another tablespoon of oil and the onion, garlic and fennel. Cook, stirring occasionally, until golden brown.

Add the anchovies, drained, and cook until they disintegrate, then add the cinnamon. Cook for another minute, then add the wine, stirring to deglaze the pan.

Return the meat to the casserole, add the tomato purée, the orange zest and juice, the rosemary and a good grinding of black pepper. Bring to a boil, reduce the heat and cover. Cook in the oven for two hours. Remove the lid and add the olives. Return to the oven for a further 20–30 minutes.

Finely chop the ingredients for the gremolata and mix together. Just before serving, stir some into the stew and sprinkle the rest on top.

Braised Featherblade with Parsley and Horseradish Dumplings

Once you discover the poor, neglected featherblade you'll be asking your butcher for it all the time. It braises beautifully, and the marbling of the meat makes for a satisfyingly rich sauce. This is one for a winter evening, or for a weekend lunch after a bracing walk on the beach or up a mountain. You can of course make it without the dumplings, but why on earth would you deprive yourself of that pleasure?

Serves 6

1.5 kg featherblade steak, cut into six portions
sea salt
black pepper
3 tablespoons extra virgin olive oil or Irish
    rapeseed oil
1 large onion, chopped
2 celery sticks, sliced
2 carrots, sliced
2 garlic cloves, crushed
250 ml red wine
500 ml beef stock
2 tablespoons tomato purée

leaves from 6 sprigs fresh thyme
1 bay leaf
1 teaspoon English mustard

FOR THE DUMPLINGS:
15 g butter
½ onion, very finely chopped
4 tablespoons finely chopped parsley
80 g breadcrumbs
1 large egg, beaten
3 heaped tablespoons creamed horseradish
    (see recipe on page 69)

Preheat the oven to 160° C/fan 140° C/gas mark 3.

Season the steak with salt and plenty of freshly ground black pepper. Heat a tablespoon of the oil in a large, heavy-bottomed casserole dish and sear the meat in batches for 2–3 minutes on each side, until nicely browned. Place the meat to one side.

Add a little more oil to the casserole dish and fry the onion, celery, carrots and garlic until softened, about ten minutes.

Return the beef to the dish and add the wine, stock, tomato purée, thyme leaves, bay leaf and mustard. Stir and bring to a simmer, then cover with a disc of greaseproof paper and the lid and place in the preheated oven. Cook for 3 hours, or until the meat is very tender.

Now make the dumplings. Melt the butter in a small frying pan, add the onion and cook over a low heat until soft. Then transfer the onions to a bowl and combine with the parsley, breadcrumbs, egg and horseradish. Form dumplings with the mixture, allowing two per person. Don't worry if they seem quite liquid – they will firm up as they cook.

Remove the beef from the oven and dot the dumplings on top. Cover and return to the oven for 20 minutes. Then remove the lid and cook for a further 10 minutes.

Serve with green vegetables. Buttered kale would be delicious.

Braised Beef Shin and Chorizo

Chorizo is one of those magic ingredients that makes virtually anything taste better. It's something worth having a supply of in the fridge, ready to be whipped out at a moment's notice. Be sure to buy it from a good delicatessen – the hard slicing chorizo in most supermarkets is a poor substitute for proper Spanish cooking chorizo.

Here it brings a delicious complexity to a very simple stew of shin beef. Any stewing cut will work in this dish, but adjust the cooking time according to the cut you use – remember, the more hard-working the muscle, the longer the cooking time. As with all slow stews and braises, a night in the fridge will only improve the flavours.

Serves 6

40 g plain flour
salt and pepper
1.5 kg shin of beef, in largish chunks
2 tablespoons extra virgin olive oil or Irish
    rapeseed oil
4 cooking chorizo sausages, removed from
    their casing and chopped into small pieces

4 carrots, chopped
3 onions, chopped
4 cloves garlic, chopped
small bunch of thyme
2 teaspoons smoked paprika
375 ml red wine, preferably Spanish
1 litre chicken stock

Preheat the oven to 140° C/fan 120° C/gas mark 1.

Season the flour with salt and pepper and dust the beef pieces in it. Brown the beef in a couple of tablespoons of the oil in a large flameproof casserole. Move the beef around as little as possible so that it picks up colour and flavour. You don't want the beef to steam, and if it catches around the edges so much the better.

Remove the beef from the pan, add another tablespoon of oil and the chorizo. Sauté until lightly coloured and remove.

Add the carrots, onions and garlic and cook until soft. Add the paprika, and return the beef and chorizo to the dish.

Add the wine and enough chicken stock to cover everything. Put in the oven for at least 3 hours until very tender. If there is too much liquid, cook for a little longer with the lid off.

Potatoes cut into small chunks and roasted with garlic, plus a big green salad, would be a fine accompaniment.

Braised Beef with Five Spice, Ginger and Highbank Apple Syrup

Highbank organic apple syrup is a truly innovative Irish ingredient. Produced by the Calder-Potts family in Co. Kilkenny, it adds a rich natural sweetness wherever it's needed. Great on porridge and pancakes, it can be used in cooking as a replacement for honey or maple syrup. It works particularly well with the subtle Asian flavours in this dish, which is adapted from a Skye Gyngell recipe.

Serves 4

1 kg braising beef, in large cubes
3 tablespoons extra virgin olive oil or Irish rapeseed oil
3 onions, peeled and finely sliced
2.5 cm piece of root ginger, peeled and finely chopped
2 red chillies, deseeded and finely chopped
3 garlic cloves, peeled and finely chopped
small bunch coriander

1 tablespoon Chinese five spice powder
2 x 400 g tins chopped tomatoes
1 litre chicken stock
50 ml fish sauce
50 ml soy sauce
5 tablespoons Highbank apple syrup (or honey or maple syrup)

Heat a couple of tablespoons of oil in a large, heavy flameproof casserole over a medium heat and cook the beef in batches until nicely browned. Do not overcrowd the pan, as the meat will steam instead and the final dish will not be as flavoursome.

Set the browned meat to one side, add another tablespoon of oil to the casserole and add the onions, ginger, chillies and garlic. Turn down the heat and cook gently until soft but not browned.

Separate the coriander leaves from the stems, and chop the stems finely. Add these to the casserole, along with the five spice powder. Cook for a couple of minutes, stirring a few times.

Return the beef to the dish, add the tomatoes and chicken stock and bring to a gentle simmer. Cook very slowly for a couple of hours until the meat is very tender. Add the fish sauce, soy sauce, and syrup and cook for another 20 minutes. Season to taste.

Garnish with the coriander leaves and serve with rice. The Asian greens on page 154 would be good too.

Barbacoa Beef Cheeks

Beef cheeks are one of our favourite cuts. The meat is intense, full of robust flavour and has a richness that is not at all cloying. Don't be put off by what might seem like a bizarre combination of ingredients; this recipe is a cinch, and it takes very little time to prepare. The recipe serves four, but our recommendation is that you make a larger batch and invite over your friends to watch a match, have a few drinks and shoot the breeze. An Irish artisan cider such as Stonewell would go nicely.

Serves 4

1 kg beef cheeks, trimmed
1 ancho chilli
4 cloves garlic, peeled and chopped
1 tablespoon peanut butter
1 teaspoon instant espresso powder
4 tablespoons extra virgin olive oil or Irish rapeseed oil
2 tablespoons Highbank apple syrup or maple syrup or honey
2 tsp ground cumin
1 tsp smoked paprika
1 handful fresh coriander, chopped
1 teaspoon salt
250 ml chicken stock

4 limes
TO SERVE:
2 avocados, peeled and sliced (or guacamole)
4 wraps or tortillas
roasted tomato salsa
fresh coriander
sour cream
grated cheese – a strongly flavoured Cheddar type such as Hegarty's from Whitechurch, Co. Cork

Remove the stem and seeds from the ancho chilli, chop it roughly and put it in a little warm water for a few minutes to rehydrate.

Blend the chilli (and its water), garlic, peanut butter, espresso powder, 2 tablespoons of the oil, syrup, cumin, paprika, coriander and salt into a paste. Marinate the beef cheeks in the paste for a few hours, preferably overnight, in the fridge.

Preheat the oven to 140° C/fan 120° C/gas mark 1½.

Heat 2 tablespoons oil in a flameproof casserole dish and brown the cheeks on both sides. Don't move the cheeks around too much when you're browning them – the less they move, the more colour and flavour they'll pick up.

Pour the rest of the marinade into the pan with the stock, then squeeze in the juice of 3 limes.

Put the lid on and place in the oven for about 3½ hours, turning the cheeks once or twice while they cook. If the liquid dries up, add a little more stock. By now the cheeks should be very tender. Pull them apart with two forks and mix with the juices in the pan. Add a squeeze of lime to taste, and a touch more syrup if you like.

Serve the barbacoa in a wrap or corn tortilla with guacamole or slices of avocado, roasted tomato salsa, sour cream, a sprinkling of fresh coriander and grated cheese.

Guacamole

2 avocados, peeled and roughly chopped
2 spring onions or ½ a small red onion, finely
    chopped
2 cloves garlic, crushed
a small bunch of coriander, chopped (leaves
    and stalks)
1 red chilli, deseeded and finely chopped
juice of ½ lime

Mash all the ingredients together.

Roast Tomato Salsa
(from Thomasina Miers)

4 plum tomatoes
1 large jalapeno chilli
2 cloves garlic
1 large tablespoon chopped coriander
½ white onion, finely chopped
juice of ½ lime
pinch of sea salt

Dry roast the tomatoes, chilli and garlic in a heavy frying pan until blackened and blistered
and soft. The tomatoes will take longer than the garlic and chilli, so remove the garlic and
chilli first.

Discard the stem of the chilli and the skin of the garlic and put the chilli and garlic in
a pestle and mortar. Pound to a paste, then add the tomatoes and work them in. Add the
coriander, onion and lime juice and season to taste.

Beef Cheeks and White Turnips in Beer with a Parsley Dressing

You've probably spotted lots of recipes for beef cheeks in this book, but you could use any braising or stewing cut for this recipe. Just keep an eye on the cooking time, which will vary according to the cut you choose.

This dish makes the most of the root vegetables that are such a fundamental part of Irish winter cooking. We have used Copper Coast Red Ale from Dungarvan Brewing, but feel free to substitute with another similar beer; any red ale would be appropriate.

Serves 6

1.5 kg large beef cheeks, trimmed
2 medium onions, quartered
2 medium carrots, quartered
2 white turnips, quartered
1 garlic bulb, halved horizontally
2 fresh thyme sprigs
1 fresh bay leaf
black peppercorns
500 ml beer
2 tablespoons extra virgin olive oil or Irish
   rapeseed oil
1 litre chicken stock

FOR THE DRESSING:
1 shallot, sliced
juice of ½ lemon
2 tablespoons extra virgin olive oil or Irish
   rapeseed oil
2 tablespoons chopped fresh flat leaf parsley

Put the beef cheeks in a large bowl with the vegetables, herbs, peppercorns and beer and marinate in the fridge for a few hours or, preferably, overnight.

Preheat the oven to 140° C/fan 120° C/gas mark 1½.

Strain the beer from the beef mixture and set aside. Season the beef cheeks with salt and freshly ground black pepper. Heat a flameproof casserole dish, add the rapeseed oil and brown the beef cheeks all over, then remove from the dish and set aside.

Reduce the heat, add the onions, carrots, turnips and garlic from the marinade and cook for 4–6 minutes, or until pale golden brown. Add the herbs and peppercorns, then add the reserved beer and continue to cook until the volume has reduced by half.

Return the beef to the dish, add the chicken stock and bring up to a simmer, cover and cook in the oven for 3 hours or until the beef is very tender.

Combine the ingredients for the dressing and serve the beef cheeks and vegetables in bowls with the dressing on top. Plain boiled potatoes would be good as an accompaniment.

Ragù: Meat Sauce, Bolognese Style

Marcella Hazan's *Classic Italian Cookbook* is one of the greats, essential in any comprehensive library of cookbooks. Hazan is credited with having introduced authentic Italian cooking to America, and her recipes are always restrained and simple. Her ragù is a no-frills version – it contains no pork and no chicken livers, no garlic and no herbs. Hazan says there are three essentials to its success: the meat is to be sautéed only long enough to lose its raw colour – it should not brown as it will lose delicacy; the milk must be added before the tomatoes to keep the meat creamy and sweet tasting; and the sauce must cook at a long and very gentle simmer – three and a half hours at least, preferably five.

Serves 6 as a modest *primi piatti*, or 3 as a more substantial main course

3 tablespoons olive oil
40 g butter
1 medium onion, chopped small
½ large stick celery, chopped small
1 medium carrot, chopped small
350 g minced beef, not too lean, preferably
　chuck

sea salt
240 ml dry white wine
120 ml milk
$^1/_8$ teaspoon freshly ground nutmeg
1 x 400 g tin chopped Italian tomatoes

In a heavy, deep cast iron casserole dish, heat the oil and butter and add the onion. Sauté briefly over a medium heat until just translucent. Add the celery and carrot and cook gently for two minutes.

Add the minced beef, crumbling it into the pot with a fork. Add one teaspoon of sea salt, stir, and cook only until the meat has lost its raw, red colour.

Add the wine, turn the heat up to medium high and cook, stirring occasionally, until all the wine has evaporated. Turn the heat down to medium, add the milk and the nutmeg. Cook until the milk has evaporated, stirring frequently. Add the tomatoes and stir thoroughly.

When the tomatoes have started to bubble, turn the heat down and cook the sauce at the laziest simmer, with just an occasional bubble.

Cook, uncovered, for at least 3½–4 hours, stirring occasionally. Taste and correct for salt.

Serve with about 50 g of spaghetti per person as a starter, or around 100 g per person as a main course.

Beef Rendang

Originally from Malaysia, rendang is a rich, dry coconut curry traditionally served with sticky rice and Asian greens. There are many variations of the recipe, but we like this version for its simplicity of preparation and deep and complex flavours. Because this is a dry curry, keep a close eye that it doesn't burn.

Serves 4

1 kg chuck or shin beef, cut into bite-sized pieces
sea salt
freshly ground black pepper
2 tablespoons groundnut oil, plus more for frying the paste
2 teaspoons cumin seeds
40 g coriander seeds
2 teaspoons turmeric
4 sticks lemongrass, outer leaf and top 5 cm of stalk removed, then chopped

4 kaffir lime leaves, shredded
2 medium onions, chopped
50 g peeled weight fresh ginger, chopped finely
4 cloves garlic, chopped finely
1–2 red chillies according to taste
850 ml stock, warmed
200 g creamed coconut

Season the beef and fry in batches in a large frying pan over a medium heat until browned. Leave to one side.

In a small, dry pan, fry the cumin seeds, coriander seeds and turmeric over a medium heat until they smell aromatic, taking care not to burn them. Grind into powder using a pestle and mortar or a spice grinder.

In a blender, combine the spices with the chopped lemongrass, kaffir lime leaves, onions, ginger, garlic and chillies, and enough of the stock (not too hot!) to make a paste.

Heat a tablespoon of groundnut oil in a heavy casserole dish and cook the paste over a medium-high heat, stirring often, for about five minutes. Add the beef, the creamed coconut and the rest of the stock.

Simmer uncovered over a low heat for about 2½ hours, stirring from time to time, or until the meat is tender. The liquid will reduce and you will be left with tender meat coated in a thick sauce.

Serve with jasmine or basmati rice and Asian greens. A pineapple relish on the side would be perfect.

Asian Greens

Heat a little groundnut oil in a wok or large frying pan. Add a 2 cm piece of ginger, peeled and finely chopped, 2 cloves of garlic, finely chopped, and 1 red chilli, finely chopped, and sauté for a minute. Add a couple of tablespoons of water or stock and 500 g mixed greens (broccoli, pak choi, spring greens, for example), adding the thicker-stemmed vegetables first. Cover and cook until tender – about 2 minutes. Season to taste with a splash or two of sesame oil and soy sauce.

Ghillie James' Pineapple, Coriander and Lime Relish

1 large ripe pineapple, peeled and cut into medium-sized chunks
2 red onions, peeled and chopped
5 cm piece fresh ginger, peeled and chopped
2 long red chillies, deseeded and chopped
2 large cloves garlic, peeled and sliced
1 small bunch coriander, stems and leaves chopped fine, but kept separate

225 g granulated sugar
225 ml white wine vinegar
juice of 3 limes
2 teaspoons fish sauce
1 teaspoon soy sauce

Put all the ingredients except the coriander leaves into a large pan and gently bring to the boil. Simmer for 1–1½ hours, stirring occasionally, until most of the liquid has evaporated and it looks syrupy. Stir in the chopped coriander leaves.

This makes about a litre. It will keep for six months if you preserve it by transferring to warm sterilised jars and sealing. Otherwise, keep it in a sealed container in the refrigerator for about a week.

Baked Beef and Almond Curry

A delicately spiced curry that needs very little attention, and does not take long to prepare.

Serves 6

4 tablespoons groundnut oil
12 small green cardamom pods
2 x 5 cm cinnamon sticks
1.2 kg stewing beef – chuck would be ideal
2 teaspoons whole cumin seeds
4 medium onions
20 g fresh ginger, finely chopped

3 tablespoons ground coriander
½ teaspoon cayenne pepper
1 teaspoon fine sea salt
500 g natural yoghurt
100 g ground almonds
juice of half a lemon

Preheat the oven to 180° C/fan 160° C/gas mark 4.

Heat the oil in a heavy ovenproof casserole and add the cardamom pods and cinnamon sticks. Brown the beef in batches, setting to one side as they are ready.

Add the cumin seeds and let them pop before adding the onions. Fry the onions until they start to turn pale brown. Add the ginger, ground coriander, cayenne and salt, and mix thoroughly with the onions.

Lower the heat and return the beef and any juices to the casserole, stir to coat the beef with the onion and spice mixture, add the yoghurt and stir to mix. Increase the heat to medium-high until the mixture reaches a simmer.

Take a large piece of foil and cover the casserole, sealing tightly around the edges. Then place the lid on top and put the casserole in the oven. Bake for about 90 minutes or until the meat is tender, adding the almonds after about an hour.

Just before serving, add lemon juice and season to taste.

Serve with basmati rice and roasted cauliflower.

Roasted Cauliflower with Cumin and Coriander

Serves 6

2 heads cauliflower
2 tablespoons cumin seeds
2 tablespoons coriander seeds
2 tablespoons groundnut oil

1 teaspoon fine sea salt
juice of ½ lemon
a handful of fresh coriander, chopped

Divide the cauliflower into florets.

Toast the cumin and coriander seeds in a dry frying pan until their aroma is released. Crush them in a mortar and pestle.

In a large bowl, toss the cauliflower with the ground cumin and coriander, the oil and salt. Place in a large tray in the oven, with the curry, until nicely browned and soft, about an hour. Just before serving, squeeze over the lemon juice and sprinkle with the chopped coriander.

Beef Shin Osso Bucco with Gremolata

Osso bucco is an Italian dish traditionally made with veal, but it is just as good (and much cheaper) made with shin beef on the bone. Cooked long and slow, this dish is the definition of comfort on a winter evening.

Serves 4

60 g plain flour
sea salt
freshly ground black pepper
4 large pieces beef shin, cut across the bone, approx. 350 g each
3 tablespoons extra virgin olive oil or Irish rapeseed oil
2 onions, chopped small
2 garlic cloves, crushed
1 carrot, chopped small
2 celery sticks, chopped small

300 ml white wine
1 x 400 g tin chopped tomatoes
400 ml beef or chicken stock
1 bay leaf

FOR THE GREMOLATA:
zest of 1 unwaxed lemon
2 garlic cloves, finely chopped
a large handful flat-leaf parsley, chopped

Preheat the oven to 150° C/fan 130° C/gas mark 2.

Put the flour on a plate, season with fine sea salt and freshly ground black pepper and dust the meat generously, coating all over.

Heat 2 tablespoons of olive oil in a large flameproof casserole, brown the meat in batches on both sides and remove to a plate.

Add another tablespoon of oil to the casserole, then add the onions, garlic, carrot and celery and cook gently for about 5 minutes until starting to soften. Add any leftover seasoned flour and stir into the vegetables. Remove from the heat and slowly add the wine.

Return the pan to the heat and simmer until the sauce has thickened slightly. Put the beef back into the pan and add the chopped tomatoes, stock and bay leaf, then season with a little fine sea salt and plenty of freshly ground black pepper. Bring to a gentle simmer, cover, then put in the oven and cook for 3 hours.

Make the gremolata by mixing the lemon zest, finely diced garlic and the parsley. Serve sprinkled on top of each shin.

The cheesy soft polenta on page 140 is a good accompaniment for this, as is the simple risotto on the next page.

Risotto Milanese

2 tablespoons extra virgin olive oil
50 g butter
1 medium onion, diced
2 litres chicken stock
1 teaspoon saffron
400 g arborio or carnaroli rice
100 ml white wine
100 g Parmesan, finely grated

In a heavy saucepan, heat the oil and half the butter over a medium heat. Add the onion and cook until translucent and soft, but not coloured.

In another saucepan, heat the chicken stock and add the saffron to the liquid.

When the onion is soft, add the rice and stir with a wooden spoon for about 4 minutes, making sure that all the grains of rice are coated with the oil/butter.

Add the wine to the rice and stir until it is all absorbed. Then add a ladle of the saffron-infused stock and cook, stirring, until it is absorbed. Continue adding the stock a ladle at a time, waiting until the liquid is absorbed before adding more.

Cook until the rice is tender and creamy and yet still a little al dente, about 15 minutes. You may not need all the stock.

Stir in the rest of the butter and half the cheese until well mixed. Serve with the rest of the cheese.

Oxtail Stew with Butternut Squash and Cinnamon

Sometimes it's hard to remember life before Ottolenghi, the London-based cafés owned by Yotam Ottolenghi and Sami Tamimi, which have been so influential over the last decade and are largely responsible for the resurgence of interest in Middle Eastern and North African cooking. This recipe appeared in their first book, *Ottolenghi: The Cookbook*.

Serves 6

2 tablespoons olive oil
2 kg oxtail pieces
200 g shallots, roughly chopped
3 large carrots, roughly chopped
2 garlic cloves, crushed
400 ml red wine
650 g Italian canned chopped tomatoes
10 sprigs of thyme
5 sprigs of rosemary

zest of ½ orange, peeled off in long strips
2 bay leaves
2 cinnamon sticks
2 star anise
1 teaspoon ground black pepper
salt
500 g butternut squash or pumpkin, peeled,
    seeded and cut into 2.5 cm cubes
300 ml water

Preheat the oven to 180° C/fan 160° C/gas mark 4.

Place a large, heavy pan over a high heat and add the olive oil. When this is smoking hot, add some of the oxtail pieces and fry on all sides for about 4 minutes, until well browned. Fry in batches so as not to overcrowd the pan. Transfer the oxtail to a colander and leave to drain off excess fat.

Remove most of the fat from the pan and add the shallots, carrots and garlic. Return to a medium-high heat and sauté, stirring occasionally, for about 10 minutes, until the vegetables are golden brown.

Add the wine to the pan and scrape the base with a wooden spoon to mix in any flavoursome bits left there. Bring to the boil and simmer until it has almost evaporated. Add the tomatoes.

Tie together the thyme and rosemary sprigs with string and drop them in as well, then add the orange zest, bay leaves, cinnamon, star anise, black pepper and some salt. Decant the simmering mixture into a deep baking dish and lay the oxtail pieces on top of the sauce in one layer (keep the pan for later).

Cover first with a sheet of baking parchment, placed directly on the oxtail, and then with a tight-fitting lid or a couple of layers of tin foil, then place in the oven and bake for 2–3 hours. The meat is ready when it comes away easily from the bone.

Lift the oxtail from the sauce, place in a large bowl and leave to cool slightly. If a lot of fat accumulates at the bottom of the bowl, decant some of it using a slotted spoon but keep the rest.

When the oxtail is cool enough to handle, pick all the meat from the bones and place back in the large pan. Add the sauce the meat was cooked in, along with the butternut squash cubes and the water.

Bring to the boil, then reduce the heat to a gentle simmer and cook for 30 minutes or until the squash is soft. Taste and season the sauce with salt and more black pepper. Transfer to a serving dish.

Serve with gremolata (see page 157) sprinkled on top.

Short Ribs with Balsamic Vinegar

Short ribs are also known as Jacob's Ladder. The flavoursome meat is well suited to slow braising; the meatier the ribs the better, so ask for them well-trimmed. Taken from the bone, short rib meat also works well in burgers.

Serves 6

6 beef short ribs, cut in half across into
  sections 5–7 cm long (allow 2 pieces (one
  rib) per person)
sea salt
freshly ground black pepper
3 tablespoons extra virgin olive oil or Irish
  rapeseed oil
6 garlic bulbs, split horizontally
4 tablespoons Highbank apple syrup (or

honey or maple syrup)
5 sprigs rosemary
1 litre balsamic vinegar (the cheap stuff is
  fine in this recipe)
110 g butter
1.6 litres chicken stock
1 litre beef stock

Season the ribs generously with fine sea salt and freshly ground black pepper. Combine the oil, garlic, apple syrup, rosemary and 250 ml of the vinegar in a bowl. Taste the marinade and if you think it needs a little more sweetness, add more syrup. Put the ribs in a Ziploc bag and add the marinade. Leave for a couple of hours, or overnight if you can.

Preheat the oven to 160° C/fan 140° C/gas mark 3.

Remove the ribs from the marinade and place in a single layer in a large oiled roasting tray. Cover with two layers of foil. Cook for about 3 hours, or until very tender, turning halfway through.

Meanwhile, make the sauce. Melt the butter in a large saucepan over medium heat. When it begins to foam, place the garlic (from the marinade) in the butter, cut side down, and cook until nicely browned but not burnt. Then add the rest of the marinade and the remaining balsamic vinegar, and cook over a high heat until reduced by about three-quarters. Add the stock and continue to cook over a high heat until starting to thicken. It should be a syrupy consistency.

Remove the ribs from the oven, pour off the juices that have accumulated, and skim off the fat from the surface. Add the skimmed juices to the sauce and reduce further if necessary. Trim any excess fat from the ribs, if you like, and coat with the sauce. Return to the oven, uncovered, and cook, turning from time to time, until nicely browned all over, about 20–30 minutes.

Braised Short Ribs with Maple Syrup and Star Anise

We've used maple syrup in this recipe but you could substitute either honey or apple syrup. Taste the marinade before you use it to make sure that it is sweet enough for your taste. Be sure to ask your butcher to trim the ribs well – you don't want them to be too fatty.

Serves 4

100 ml light soy sauce
300 ml cloudy apple juice
150 ml maple syrup
1 tablespoon sesame oil
4 large cloves garlic, unpeeled and smashed
　 with the flat of a knife
10 peppercorns
4 star anise
4 beef short ribs (one rib per person), cut in
　 half across and well trimmed

First make the marinade by combining the soy sauce, apple juice, maple syrup and sesame oil in a saucepan and bringing it to the boil. Stir until everything is well mixed together. Add the garlic cloves, peppercorns and star anise to the marinade. Turn off the heat and leave to cool.

Marinate the ribs in the fridge in a covered bowl or large Ziploc bag for at least 24 hours, turning a couple of times. Longer won't do any harm.

Preheat the oven to 160° C/fan 140° C/gas mark 3. Put the ribs and marinade into a roasting tin and cover with a double layer of foil. Roast for about 3 hours or until the meat is tender, turning once or twice during cooking.

Drain off the juices and skim the fat from the surface. Transfer the juices to a saucepan and reduce over a high heat until they reach a syrupy consistency, taking care not to burn the sauce. Trim any excess fat from the ribs, if you like, then pour the sauce over the ribs and return to the oven to cook, uncovered, turning a few times, until browned all over, about 20–30 minutes.

Thai Red Beef Curry

Serves 4

800 g sirloin steak, cut into strips
3 tablespoons red Thai curry paste
3 cloves garlic, finely chopped
8 cm piece of ginger, finely chopped
1 teaspoon sesame oil
3 tablespoons groundnut oil
3 spring onions, finely sliced
200 ml coconut milk
250 ml chicken stock

2 teaspoons Thai fish sauce (nam pla)
2 heads pak choi, chopped
1 teaspoon lime juice
1–2 teaspoons honey (optional)
4 tablespoons coriander, chopped

In a bowl, combine the strips of beef with half the red curry paste, half the garlic, half the ginger and all the sesame oil.

Heat 2 tablespoons of groundnut oil in a wok over a high heat and stir fry the beef rapidly until just cooked. This will take about 3 minutes. Fry the beef in batches rather than overcrowding the wok as the meat will steam rather than fry and the flavour of the finished dish will not be as good. Set the cooked beef to one side.

Add another tablespoon of groundnut oil to the wok and fry the sliced spring onions for a minute, then add the rest of the curry paste. Add the coconut milk, chicken stock and fish sauce and bring to the boil. Reduce to a simmer and add the pak choi. After a minute, return the beef to the sauce and simmer for another minute.

Add lime juice to taste, and if you like your curry to have a little sweetness, add a teaspoon or two of honey.

Sprinkle with chopped coriander and serve with steamed jasmine rice or rice noodles.

Very Slow Beef Shin

In the village of Panzano in northern Tuscany, Dario Cecchini is a butcher who also has a restaurant, Solociccia (meaning 'only meat'), that serves the traditional local recipe, Peposo alla Fornacina, in which beef shin on the bone is cooked at a very low temperature for a long time. This interpretation is from River Café in London. It couldn't be simpler.

Serves 6

3 kg beef shin on the bone, cut across the
  shin
1 bottle Chianti Classico (have another on
  standby)
50 garlic cloves, peeled
8 sprigs thyme
3 tablespoons ground black pepper
sea salt
extra virgin olive oil
sourdough bread

Preheat the oven to 70° C/fan 50° C/the lowest gas setting.

Place the beef in a large casserole dish with a close-fitting lid. Cover with the wine and add the garlic, thyme, pepper and a little salt. Slowly bring to the boil, then cover with greaseproof paper. Put the lid on and cook in the preheated oven for 12 hours.

Take a look every four hours and top up the wine if the liquid isn't covering the beef. Test for seasoning.

Cut the bread into thick slices and toast on both sides. Serve chunks of meat on top of the toast with the garlic and juices, drizzled with olive oil.

Braised Oxtail in Red Wine

Oxtail is rich and satisfying, and this very simple recipe is comfort in a bowl. You could use any leftover meat to make the oxtail and truffle pizza on page 199.

Serves 4

150 ml extra virgin olive oil or Irish
   rapeseed oil
1.5 kg oxtail
75 g plain flour
4 garlic cloves, peeled and finely sliced
3 large shallots, peeled and finely chopped
2 carrots, peeled and roughly chopped
2 leeks, white part only, washed and finely
   chopped

2 sticks celery, peeled and roughly chopped
4 bay leaves
small bunch fresh thyme
flaky sea salt
freshly ground black pepper
1 bottle red wine
2 litres chicken stock

Heat 3 tablespoons of the oil in a heavy flameproof casserole. Dip the pieces of oxtail in the flour so that they are fully coated. Fry the oxtail in the oil for about five minutes on each side, until browned. Set aside and drain on kitchen paper.

Add some more oil to the pan and fry the garlic and shallots gently for a couple of minutes. Add the carrots, leeks and celery and stir well. Cook for another minute, then add the bay leaves, thyme, a good pinch of salt and plenty of freshly ground black pepper.

Return the oxtail to the casserole and add the wine and chicken stock. Bring to the boil, then turn the heat down to a gentle simmer, cover and cook for about 3 hours over a low heat, or until the meat is tender.

Remove the meat and place to one side, then skim the fat from the sauce and simmer over a medium heat until reduced to a thick consistency. Return the oxtail to the pan, heat through and serve in bowls with creamy mashed potato or champ.

Moroccan Tagine with Preserved Lemons

If you are in search of a crowd-pleasing main course that you can prepare ahead of time, look no further. We like to serve this with a vibrant herby couscous (coriander, mint and flat-leaf parsley are all good), to which we add the juice and zest of a couple of lemons, a little olive oil and plenty of flaky sea salt and freshly ground black pepper. A roasted carrot and orange salad (see page 170) is a perfect accompaniment.

Serves 12

6 tablespoons extra virgin olive oil or Irish
   rapeseed oil
5 medium onions, sliced
4 large cloves garlic, sliced
2.6 kg shin of beef or other stewing cut,
   cubed
sea salt and black pepper
½ teaspoon chilli flakes
3 bay leaves
1 tablespoon cardamom pods, crushed and
   husks discarded
3 tablespoons ground coriander
¾ teaspoon ground nutmeg
1½ teaspoons ginger
1½ teaspoons turmeric
large pinch saffron

2 cinnamon sticks
1½ tablespoons Highbank apple syrup or
   honey
1.6 litres chicken stock
700 g butternut squash, cubed
300 g chickpeas, soaked overnight and
   simmered until tender
300 g dried apricots, chopped
1½ preserved lemons, skin only, chopped
100 g pine nuts, toasted

FOR THE GREMOLATA:
large bunch coriander, chopped
2 preserved lemons, skin only, chopped
   finely

In a very large, heavy saucepan, or two smaller ones, sauté the onions and garlic in a couple of tablespoons of oil over a low heat until soft and starting to brown.

Season the beef with plenty of sea salt and black pepper. In a large frying pan, heat another couple of tablespoons of oil and fry the beef in batches until nicely browned. Remove the browned beef to a bowl.

When the onions and garlic are soft, add the beef, chilli flakes, bay leaves, cardamom seeds, coriander, nutmeg, ginger, turmeric, saffron and cinnamon sticks and stir well so that the spices are well distributed.

Add the apple syrup or honey and the chicken stock and simmer, covered, over a low heat until the meat is tender but not falling apart. Add the butternut squash and continue to simmer until it too is almost tender, but not squishy.

Add the chickpeas, apricots and preserved lemon skin and simmer, uncovered, for another 10 minutes. Taste and season with sea salt and black pepper. Allowed to cool and refrigerated overnight, this will be even better the next day.

To make the gremolata, combine the chopped coriander and the preserved lemon skins.

Serve the tagine in bowls with the gremolata and some toasted pine nuts sprinkled on top.

Roasted Carrot and Orange Salad

Serves 12

12 medium carrots, peeled
2 teaspoons each cumin seeds, coriander
    seeds and fennel seeds
75 ml extra virgin olive oil or Irish
    rapeseed oil
1 teaspoon flaky sea salt
½ teaspoon cayenne pepper
6 oranges (use blood oranges if they're in
    season)
3 garlic cloves, minced
juice of 1 lemon
2 handfuls rocket
50 g black olives, pitted and chopped

Preheat the oven to 220° C/fan 200° C/gas mark 7.

Cut the carrots lengthwise into quarters and then into 5 cm chunks.

Crush the cumin, coriander and fennel seeds in a pestle and mortar.

Toss the carrots with 3 tablespoons of oil, the crushed spices, ¾ teaspoon salt and the cayenne pepper, and roast, shaking the tin occasionally, until tender and caramelised, which will take between 30 and 40 minutes. Allow to cool to room temperature.

Grate the zest of 1 orange into a small bowl and add the garlic, ¼ teaspoon salt, the lemon juice and 2 tablespoons of oil.

Slice the tops and bottoms from each orange and peel them, using a sharp knife, being sure to get rid of all the pith. Holding each orange over a large bowl, slice away the fruit between the membranes, releasing the segments into the bowl.

Toss the carrots, rocket and olives into the bowl with the dressing. Taste and add more salt and lemon juice if necessary.

Stracotto

Stracotto is basically the Italian version of the French daube, for which there is a recipe on page 99.

Serves 6

5 tablespoons extra virgin olive oil
200 g pancetta, cubed
1.5 kg stewing beef, cubed
2 onions, chopped
5 large cloves garlic, smashed
2 bay leaves
1 teaspoon chopped fresh oregano, or ½
   teaspoon dried
1 cinnamon stick
½ teaspoon ground cloves

3 carrots, roughly chopped
zest of ½ lemon, in strips
flaky sea salt
freshly ground black pepper
3 tablespoons plain flour
3 tablespoons tomato purée
200 ml red wine
500 ml chicken stock
2 tablespoons aged balsamic vinegar

Heat 2 tablespoons of the oil in a heavy casserole dish and cook the pancetta until browned. Transfer it to a dish and set aside.

Add the beef to the pan in batches, taking care not to overcrowd the pan, and cook until browned. Transfer the beef to the dish with the pancetta.

Add 2 more tablespoons of the oil to the pan and stir in the onion, garlic, bay leaves, oregano, cinnamon stick, cloves, carrots and lemon zest. Sauté until the vegetables are lightly coloured.

Return the beef and pancetta to the pan, season with salt and pepper, and stir. Sprinkle the flour over the meat. Stir in the tomato purée, then the wine and enough chicken stock just to cover the meat.

Cover and cook over a low heat, stirring occasionally, until the meat is tender, probably about 2 hours. Add a little more chicken stock during cooking if it starts to dry out. Add the balsamic vinegar and season to taste.

Chapter 6
Burgers, Brisket, Meatballs & Dude Food

Over the past few years, there's been a revival in the kind of gutsy food and big flavours that we associate with honest to goodness, straightforward American cooking. Making a great burger isn't complicated – in fact it couldn't be easier – and once you've crafted your own, you will never again think about picking up a packet from the freezer cabinet; there's just no comparison.

There's a trend too for restaurants and food trucks that smoke, barbecue and pull their meat. Most of these techniques can be carried out at home and they produce seriously tasty food that makes the most of some under-utilised cuts.

The dishes in this chapter work particularly well with the terrific craft beers and ciders now produced in Ireland, so take the opportunity to try some of them the next time you cook some of these crowd-pleasing recipes.

Absolutely Simple 100% Beef Burgers with Optional Bone Marrow

For the perfect burger, don't get meat that's too lean – you need some fat for lubrication. For a succulent burger, we reckon the perfect ratio of meat to fat is 80:20. Some cuts, such as chuck, short rib and cheek, naturally have about 20% fat, so there's no need to introduce extra fat if you use one of these. Heston Blumenthal recommends a ratio of 2:1:1 of chuck, short rib and brisket, which is definitely worth trying if you are catering for a crowd. If you use a leaner cut, such as sirloin or flank, you can supplement the lean meat with bone marrow to achieve the desired 80:20 ratio. Adding bone marrow makes for a ridiculously flavoursome burger. If you're not sure about the percentage of fat in the cut of meat that you're thinking about using, ask your butcher's advice. And make sure you get coarsely ground mince; it makes a huge difference to the texture and flavour of the finished burger. Burgers taste better when they are served medium rare – that's a fact. But the advice is that children, elderly people and anyone with a compromised immune system should eat their burgers cooked through. It's advisable to have the meat minced to order and to use it the same day.

Makes 6 burgers

1.2 kg chuck steak, short rib or cheek,
   coarsely minced
or 1 kg rump or flank steak, coarsely minced,
   and 200 g bone marrow, chopped into 1 cm
   cubes
flaky sea salt
freshly ground black pepper

Form the meat into six thick disc-shaped burgers, and press a dimple into the centre of each to help them to keep their shape while cooking. Cover and chill for an hour so that the burgers will retain their shape and hold together during cooking.

Preheat a heavy, cast iron ridged grill pan or barbecue until smoking. Just before you place the burgers on the grill, season with sea salt flakes and freshly ground black pepper.

There is no need to oil either the grill or the burger, as the fat content of the meat will prevent the burger sticking, but if you are concerned that it might stick (because you have used very lean meat), brush the meat with a light coating of rapeseed oil before seasoning.

Place on the grill and cook for four minutes. Flip and cook the other side, until the burgers are nicely charred. The interior will still be pink, but you can cook them for longer if you prefer your burger well done.

Knockmealdown Burgers

For a burger with the flavour of sweet caramelised onions, try this recipe using Knockmealdown porter, one of our favourite craft beers, produced by Eight Degrees in the beautiful Ballyhoura region of Co. Cork.

Makes 6 burgers

1 tablespoon rapeseed oil
1 large onion, finely chopped
1 kg coarsely ground beef mince (80:20 ratio
   of meat to fat)
100 ml Eight Degrees Knockmealdown stout
2 tablespoons brown breadcrumbs
2 teaspoons finely chopped parsley and/or
   thyme
1 teaspoon sea salt
freshly ground black pepper

Heat the oil in a frying pan over a low heat and fry the onion slowly for about 20 minutes, until soft and slightly browned. Leave to cool.

Combine the beef with the onion, stout, breadcrumbs, herbs and seasoning. Divide the meat mixture into six, and form into flat burgers, pressing a dimple into the centre of each, which will help them to remain flat during cooking.

Cover and chill for an hour so that the burgers will retain their shape and hold together during cooking.

Cook on the barbecue, or on a heavy, cast iron ridged griddle pan preheated to smoking. There is no need to oil either the grill or the burgers, but if you are concerned that they might stick (because you have used very lean meat), lightly brush the burgers with oil. Place on the grill for about 4 minutes per side for medium rare.

Good Things to Eat with Burgers

You probably don't need us to tell you what to put on your burger.

You won't go far wrong, of course, with lettuce, tomato and a slice of raw onion. Tomato ketchup, mayonnaise and American yellow mustard are all traditional and, some would say, essential. A slice of cheese is good, but instead of generic slices of processed 'Cheddar', try an Irish artisan cheese such as Smoked Bay Lough or Cooleeney, both wonderful local cheeses produced in Tipperary. Or maybe some crisp organic bacon from Crowe's outdoor-reared pigs or from the happy whey-fed porkers raised by the Ferguson family, whose Gubbeen brand has long been associated with the highest standards of artisan food production in Ireland.

If you need further inspiration, here are a few suggestions for accompaniments to make your burger sing even louder.

Mayonnaise/Aïoli

Home-made mayonnaise is another story entirely from the shop-bought version. Experiment with various oils – some olive or rapeseed oils on their own may be too strongly flavoured for your taste, and will work better combined with a flavourless oil such as groundnut.

3 egg yolks
2 teaspoons Dijon mustard
pinch sea salt
cold water
1 tablespoon lemon juice
700 ml oil
2 cloves garlic (for aïoli)

Combine the egg yolks, mustard, salt, one tablespoon each of water and lemon juice in a food processer, if you have one, or whisk in a bowl. Mix thoroughly, and then add the oil slowly, drop by drop at first so that the mayonnaise doesn't curdle, until the consistency is right.

Grate in the garlic to make aïoli.

Charred Spring Onion Sour Cream

20 spring onions
extra virgin olive oil or Irish rapeseed oil
120 ml aïoli or mayonnaise

450 ml sour cream
smoked sea salt
black pepper

Clean the spring onions and cut off the root ends. Coat them generously with oil and salt and place them on a hot grill or barbecue. Grill until very well charred.

Mince the charred scallions and mix with the aïoli (or mayonnaise) and sour cream. Add smoked salt and black pepper to taste.

Coriander Aïoli

2 large bunches coriander
2 cloves of garlic, peeled and crushed
230 ml extra virgin olive oil or Irish
   rapeseed oil

juice of 1 lime, or more to taste
pinch of sea salt
450 ml aïoli or mayonnaise

Blend the coriander, garlic, oil, lime juice and sea salt together until puréed. Add the purée to aïoli or mayonnaise.

Confit Garlic

Be sure to buy good fat heads of garlic for this recipe – peeling small cloves will drive you demented.

500 g whole garlic cloves, peeled
1 teaspoon sea salt
about 400 ml extra virgin olive oil or Irish
   rapeseed oil

Place the garlic cloves and salt in a small saucepan, and just cover them with oil. Simmer on a low heat. Once the garlic cloves are soft and squishy, allow them to cool and transfer to the fridge. They will keep indefinitely if covered with oil and are great as a pizza topping, as well as in sandwiches or crammed into burgers. You can make confit cherry tomatoes the same way – just add a few sprigs of fresh rosemary or thyme to the oil.

Chilli con Carne

There used to be a restaurant in New York called Exterminator Chili, with its signature dish graded according to the likelihood of its blowing your head off. On offer were residential (mild), commercial (hot), industrial (extremely hot), and agricultural (veggie) strength. Our recipe isn't especially fiery, but by all means feel free to up the heat quotient according to your personal taste.

This chilli is even better left overnight and reheated the next day.

Serves 6–8

2 tablespoons extra virgin olive oil or Irish rapeseed oil
1 kg chuck steak, chopped by hand into very small pieces
2 onions, thinly sliced
5 cloves of garlic, finely chopped
500 ml coffee
2 tablespoons chipotle paste

1 teaspoon flaky sea salt
1 teaspoon cumin seeds, toasted
1 tablespoon oregano
2 tablespoons Highbank apple syrup (or honey, or maple syrup)
1 teaspoon chilli flakes, or to taste
1 fresh green chilli, finely chopped
400 g cooked kidney beans

Heat the oil in a large, heavy-bottomed pan over a medium-high heat, and then brown the meat, in batches if necessary. Set the meat to one side.

Add the onions to the pan and cook until lightly browned. Add the garlic and cook until the onion and garlic are completely softened

Return the meat to the pan, add the coffee and a generous pinch of salt and simmer, covered, for 2 hours.

Add the chipotle paste, salt, cumin seeds and oregano to the meat along with the Highbank syrup (or honey, or maple syrup), chilli flakes and fresh chilli and simmer, partially covered, for another 30 minutes. Add a little water or stock if it is too dry.

Add the beans, cook for a further 10 minutes, taste, and adjust the seasoning and spicing if necessary.

Serve with sour cream, grated cheese and chopped avocado and tomato. Instead of rice on the side, think about trying the easy cornbread opposite.

Quick Buttermilk Cornbread

1½ teaspoons sea salt
650 g cornmeal
4 tablespoons plain flour
6 teaspoons baking powder
2 teaspoons ground cinnamon
750 ml buttermilk

4 eggs
2 teaspoons Highbank apple syrup (or honey, or maple syrup)
4 tablespoons sunflower oil

Preheat the oven to 200° C/fan 180° C/gas mark 6.

Combine the salt, cornmeal, flour, baking powder and cinnamon in a bowl. Whisk together the buttermilk, eggs, syrup (or honey) and oil, and then stir into the dry ingredients. Mix well.

Grease a rectangular cake tin (23 cm x 20 cm approx.) and pour in the cornbread batter. Bake in the preheated oven for 30 minutes or until the cornbread has risen.

Cut the cornbread into squares and serve.

Brined Beef Brisket on the Bone with Barbecue Sauce

This recipe is a labour of love that takes time but is well worth it. Do make it with a fine big piece of brisket so that you get the most out of your efforts. Brining the meat makes it very moist and juicy, but the recipe for slow-cooked pulled chipotle brisket (page 186) is very good too, and takes less preparation time.

Serves 10

4 kg piece of brisket on the bone
yellow mustard

FOR THE BRINE:
1 litre apple juice
750 ml water
600 g sugar
200 g sea salt
200 ml Worcestershire sauce

FOR THE DRY RUB:
4 tablespoons smoked paprika
4 tablespoons sea salt
2 tablespoons sugar
1 tablespoon freshly ground black pepper
1 teaspoon turmeric
2 tablespoons garlic powder
2 tablespoons dried thyme

FOR THE BARBECUE SAUCE:
250 ml cider vinegar
250 ml balsamic vinegar
500 ml water
150 g tomato purée
1 medium onion, chopped
I thick slice of lemon
50 ml Worcestershire sauce
8 tablespoons honey
8 tablespoons treacle
1 teaspoon chilli flakes
2 bay leaves
½ teaspoon freshly ground black pepper
400 g brown sugar
2 tablespoons yellow mustard
2 tablespoons tomato ketchup
4 cloves garlic, peeled and crushed
2 tablespoons sea salt

First make the brine. Place all the ingredients in a saucepan over a high heat and stir while bringing to the boil. Remove from the heat and stir until the sugar and salt are completely dissolved. Leave to cool.

Place the brisket in the brine for a couple of hours, choosing a container that allows you to submerge the meat completely.

Make the dry rub by combining all the ingredients. Remove the brisket from the brine and pat dry with kitchen paper. Smear the surface of the brisket with yellow mustard. Then sprinkle all over with the dry rub.

If you have a stove-top smoker, put in the brisket for about an hour over medium heat, checking it every so often to make sure that the meat does not burn. This step is optional – there's no need to rush out and buy a smoker – it just adds an extra dimension.

Make the barbecue sauce by putting all the ingredients into a large pot over high heat. Bring

to the boil, reduce the heat and simmer for about 1 hour and 15 minutes or until the consistency is sauce-like. Remove the bay leaves and lemon and blend with a hand blender.

Preheat the oven to 130° C/fan 110° C/gas mark 1.

Place the brisket in a roasting tray and cover with a layer of clingfilm and two layers of tinfoil. Cook in the preheated oven for approximately five hours, or until very tender. To char the outside, either finish the brisket on the barbecue or in the oven with the foil off until it is nicely browned and the fat is crisp.

When the brisket is cool enough to handle, extract the meat, the crisp fat and the outer bark from the surface, discarding any excess visible fat. Combine with the barbecue sauce, warm gently, and serve with red slaw and sweet potato wedges (see 187).

Slow-Cooked Pulled Chipotle Brisket

A simpler version of the brisket recipe above, in which overnight marinating takes the place of the brining.

Serves 6

2 kg piece of brisket, on the bone

FOR THE MARINADE:
6 tablespoons tomato purée
2 tablespoons chipotle paste
330 ml beer
2 tablespoons wine vinegar
2 tablespoons Worcestershire sauce

2 tablespoons Highbank apple syrup (or honey, or maple syrup)
2 tablespoons Dijon mustard
small bunch of thyme
4 cloves of garlic, smashed
freshly ground black pepper
sea salt

Combine all the ingredients for the marinade. Slather the marinade all over the meat and place in the fridge, covered with clingfilm, overnight.

The next day, place the brisket and marinade in a roasting dish and cover well with tin foil. Cook at 130° C/fan 110° C/ gas mark 1 for about 5 hours or until the meat is very tender and falling apart. Cook for a further 30 minutes without the foil, until the meat is nicely browned.

When the joint is cool enough to handle, remove any excess fat and shred the meat. Pour the cooking liquid, along with any interesting bits of caramelised sauce, into a jug and allow the fat to rise to the top. Skim off the fat, reduce the juices if they are very liquid, and add the pulled meat to the remaining juices. Serve in a bap with red slaw.

Red Slaw

Serves 6

¼ red cabbage
1 bulb fennel, trimmed
2 large carrots, peeled
2 large beetroot, peeled
1 bunch spring onions, trimmed
1 large bunch of coriander, chopped
125 ml natural yoghurt
125 ml mayonnaise
juice of 1 lime

Finely slice the cabbage and fennel, and grate the carrots and beetroot. Slice the spring onions finely. Combine in a bowl with the chopped coriander.

Make a dressing with the yoghurt, mayonnaise and lime juice and add to the vegetables.

Sweet Potato Wedges

Serves 6

6 medium sweet potatoes
extra virgin olive oil or Irish rapeseed oil
2 teaspoons ground cumin

Preheat the oven to 200° C/fan 180° C/gas mark 6.

Slice the sweet potatoes lengthwise into wedges. Brush the slices with oil and sprinkle with ground cumin. Lay on a sheet of greaseproof paper and place in the oven for about 45 minutes or until tender and starting to caramelise.

Spanish Meatballs in a Tomato Chorizo Sauce

Baking the meatballs in the oven rather than frying them makes this recipe very straightforward and the chorizo elevates the dish from run of the mill to something a little more special with very little extra effort. This is a terrific multi-generational crowd-pleaser; the quantities can be easily doubled for a larger number.

Serves 10

1 kg minced beef
250 g minced free range pork
1 onion, finely chopped
large handful of flat-leaf parsley, finely
  chopped
2 tablespoons smoked sweet paprika
100 g fresh breadcrumbs
2 eggs, beaten
fine sea salt
freshly ground black pepper
extra virgin olive oil or Irish rapeseed oil

FOR THE SAUCE:
200 g cooking chorizo, stripped from its skin
  and finely chopped
2 tablespoons extra virgin olive oil or Irish
  rapeseed oil
4 cloves of garlic, crushed
4 x 400 g tins chopped tomatoes
125 ml red wine
1 tablespoon caster sugar
large handful of flat-leaf parsley, finely
  chopped

Preheat the oven to 220° C/fan 200° C/gas mark 7.

Combine the ingredients for the meatballs in a large bowl, using your hands to ensure that everything is evenly distributed. Form the mixture into balls about the size of a golf ball. You should have around 50 in total.

Brush a large roasting tin with a little olive oil and place the meatballs on the tray, then drizzle with a little more olive oil. Bake in the in the oven for about half an hour, shaking the tin from time to time, until the meatballs are evenly browned. If they catch a little and start to caramelise, so much the better.

Once the meatballs are in the oven, heat a frying pan over a medium heat and fry the chorizo until browned. The chorizo will release fat as it cooks, so there is no need to add any to the pan.

Heat the oil in a large, heavy-bottomed pan. Add the garlic and let it fry for a couple of minutes until golden. Add the tomatoes, wine and sugar. Season generously and bring to a simmer. Simmer, stirring from time to time, until it has thickened slightly, which will take about half an hour.

Add the chorizo and the fat that it has released during cooking to the tomato sauce and stir. Add the parsley and check the seasoning. Add the cooked meatballs to the pan and coat them with the sauce.

Serve with rice, herbed couscous or cubed roast potatoes, and a green salad.

Chapter 7
Pasta &
Pizza

Life's too short to eat gloopy lasagne, particularly when it's so easy for it to be very, very good. And so very, very comforting. It's one of those dishes that should be in everyone's repertoire.

As for pizza, why order in when it's so simple to make remarkable ones at home? The suggestions here are just the start of what we predict will be a long and happy voyage of discovery with home-made pizza. The toppings would work just as well on slices of griddled sourdough for bruschetta.

Classic Lasagne

Lasagne is one of those dishes that everyone should know how to make. And everyone thinks they do – but we all know that's not true. An eligible widower friend in the USA says that it was only when his wife died that he came to appreciate how truly wonderful her version of the classic lasagne was, when compared to the abominations that came his way in the name of sympathy, usually in a container helpfully marked with the name and number of the cook! Here we use the ragù recipe from page 150, but by all means experiment with it, perhaps incorporating some minced pork or diced pancetta, or some chopped herbs–a little finely chopped rosemary is a great addition. But please leave out the peppers and mushrooms. Really, they have no place in this dish. You can make a lighter and quicker version with an alternative to the traditional béchamel – see below.

Serves 6–8

70 g butter
40 g plain flour
1 litre milk
1 teaspoons sea salt
1 teaspoon freshly grated nutmeg
extra virgin olive oil or Irish rapeseed oil
2 x ragù recipe (page 150)
250 g fresh lasagne sheets
100 g finely grated Parmesan

Preheat the oven to 200° C/fan 180° C/gas mark 6.

First make the béchamel sauce. Heat the butter in a medium saucepan over low heat until melted. Add the flour and stir until smooth. Cook over a medium heat for about 6 to 7 minutes.

Meanwhile, heat the milk in a separate pan until just about to boil. Gradually add the hot milk to the butter and flour mixture, whisking continuously until very smooth. Bring to a boil. Cook for 10 minutes, stirring constantly, then remove from the heat. Season with salt and nutmeg, and set aside until ready to use.

Brush the bottom and sides of a lasagne dish with oil. Lay a couple of the fresh lasagne sheets on the bottom of the dish. Spread a layer of the meat sauce over the pasta, and then pour on a layer of béchamel sauce. Sprinkle with a little finely grated Parmesan. Repeat the layers, ending up with a pasta layer, over which you spread the remaining béchamel and a final sprinkling of cheese.

Bake in the oven for about 45 minutes or until heated through and nicely browned on top.

Alternative to béchamel: combine 500 ml crème fraîche with 3 finely chopped anchovies, 150 g finely grated Parmesan and enough milk to make the sauce of pouring consistency, but not too thin. Use in place of the béchamel.

Irish Beef Cheek Lasagne

This was one of our great discoveries when we were testing recipes for this book. It elevates the humble lasagne to another level entirely.

Serves 6–8

70 g butter
40 g plain flour
1 litre milk
1 teaspoon salt
1 teaspoon freshly grated nutmeg
extra virgin olive oil or Irish rapeseed oil
½ quantity multi-tasking meat sauce (see the
  recipe on page 139)

250 g fresh lasagne sheets
100 g finely grated hard Irish cheese–Coolea,
  Cratloe Hills, Desmond or Hegarty's
  Cheddar will all work well–or the
  traditional Parmesan

Preheat the oven to 200° C/fan 180° C/gas mark 6.

First make the béchamel sauce. Heat the butter in a medium saucepan over a low heat until melted. Add the flour and stir until smooth. Cook for about 6 to 7 minutes over a medium heat. Meanwhile, heat the milk in a separate pan until just about to boil. Gradually add the hot milk to the butter and flour mixture, whisking continuously until very smooth. Bring to a boil. Cook for 10 minutes, stirring constantly, then remove from the heat. Season with salt and nutmeg, and set aside until ready to use.

Brush the bottom and sides of a lasagne dish with oil. Lay a couple of the fresh lasagne sheets on the bottom of the dish. Spread a layer of the meat sauce over the pasta, and then pour on a layer of béchamel sauce. Sprinkle with a little finely grated cheese. Repeat the layers, ending up with a pasta layer, over which you spread the remaining béchamel and a final sprinkling of cheese.

Bake in the oven for about 45 minutes or until hot through and nicely browned on top.

Beef, Spinach and Toons Bridge Ricotta Cannelloni

How wonderful that we now have Irish ricotta, produced in Co. Cork from the milk of buffalo with Irish passports.

Serves 6

2 onions, finely chopped
120 ml extra virgin olive oil
500 g minced beef
sea salt
freshly ground black pepper
450 g fresh spinach, thick stalks discarded
700 g Toons Bridge or other ricotta cheese
150 g mascarpone
¼ teaspoon grated nutmeg

300 g Desmond or Parmesan cheese, 200 g grated and 100 g shaved
500 g cannelloni tubes, dried or fresh
2 x 400 g tins chopped Italian tomatoes
small bunch of fresh basil, leaves only
160 ml double cream

Preheat the oven to 200° C/fan 180° C/gas mark 6.

Fry the onion in 2 tablespoons of the olive oil until golden. Add the beef and season with sea salt and freshly ground black pepper. Cook for about 10–15 minutes. Leave the meat to cool.

In the meantime, cook the spinach, covered, in a little boiling water until wilted. Drain and allow to cool, then squeeze out any excess water and chop finely.

When the meat and spinach have cooled, mix them with the ricotta, mascarpone, nutmeg and grated cheese. Taste the mixture and season. If using dried pasta, cook the cannelloni tubes according to the packet instructions, then fill with the meat and spinach mixture and place in a greased, deep-sided baking tray. Fresh tubes will not need pre-cooking.

When all the tubes are in the tray, cover with the chopped tomatoes, basil and cream. Season again and drizzle over a couple more tablespoons of extra virgin olive oil. Cover with foil and bake for about 10 minutes, then remove the foil and bake for a further 10 minutes until hot through and bubbling. Serve topped with the shaved cheese.

Bone Marrow Pizza

The bone marrow gives a rich beefiness to this pizza – you might not manage a whole one on your own, so is perhaps best shared between two as a starter, or cut into small pieces as part of an antipasti offering. The Irish-made pizza bases sold under the Pizza da Piero brand are excellent and the mozzarella produced by Toby Simmonds and John Lynch in Co. Cork – with the help of their herd of buffalo, of course – is a genuinely innovative Irish product that stands up to comparison with the best buffalo mozzarella from Italy.

Makes 1 pizza

extra virgin olive oil or Irish rapeseed oil
2 shallots, finely sliced
3 large cloves garlic, finely sliced
1 pizza base
½ ball Toons Bridge Irish mozzarella or
    other buffalo mozzarella
50 g bone marrow, chopped

3 tablespoons finely grated hard cheese –
    Hegarty's, Desmond, Coolea, Cratloe Hills
    or Parmesan
1 tablespoon finely chopped parsley
small handful of caper berries

Preheat the oven to its highest setting.

In a small frying pan, heat a tablespoon of oil and gently fry the shallots and garlic until soft and golden. Tear the mozzarella into small pieces and dot evenly over the surface of the pizza. Add the shallots and garlic, with their oil, and distribute evenly over the pizza. Add the chopped bone marrow and finally sprinkle with the hard cheese.

Place on a heated oven tray or pizza stone in the preheated oven until bubbling and starting to brown. Sprinkle the pizza with a little finely chopped parsley and scatter the caper berries over the top.

Oxtail and Truffle Pizza

This is another unusual and delicious pizza that makes a wonderfully stylish starter for a kitchen supper with friends. It's a great way of using up those little jars of truffle paste and bottles of truffle oil that you buy on holiday in France or Italy and then leave to languish at the back of the cupboard. And it's a reason to keep a little oxtail in reserve whenever you cook it.

Makes 1 pizza

1 pizza base (try the Irish Pizza da Piero brand)
1 tablespoon truffle paste or truffle butter
10 cloves of confit garlic (see the recipe on page 178)
½ ball Toons Bridge Irish mozzarella or other buffalo mozzarella
100 g cooked oxtail (see the recipe on page 167)

3 tablespoons finely grated hard cheese – Hegarty's, Desmond, Coolea, Cratloe Hills, or Parmesan
handful of rocket leaves
1 tablespoon truffle oil
flaky sea salt

Preheat the oven to its highest setting.

Spread the truffle paste or butter in a thin layer over the pizza base. Squish the confit garlic with the back of a spoon and distribute across the pizza. Tear the mozzarella into small pieces and dot evenly over the top. Shred the oxtail with your fingers and add to the pizza. Finally, sprinkle with the hard cheese.

Place on a heated oven tray or pizza stone and cook in the preheated oven until bubbling and starting to brown. Serve with the rocket strewn across the pizza and drizzled with the truffle oil and a little flaky sea salt.

Chapter 8
Pies

There's something about a pie that exudes generosity and abundance. Perhaps because they are perceived as difficult or time-consuming, and aren't made at home as often as they used to be, the sight of a big pie being brought straight from the oven to the table is one that elicits sighs of pleasure and anticipation.

Steak, Kidney and Mushroom Pie with a Marrowbone Funnel

This is a real showstopper, almost medieval in appearance. We've given a recipe for a rich bone marrow pastry, which is truly delicious, but you can use ready-made puff or savoury shortcrust, as long as it is an 'all butter' version. We won't tell. The Irish brand Roll It is excellent.

Serves 6

FOR THE PASTRY:
500 g self-raising flour
5 g baking powder
the leaves from 4 sprigs of thyme
fine sea salt
freshly ground black pepper
100 g bone marrow, chilled and grated
100 g butter, chilled and grated
4 egg yolks
ice-cold milk

FOR THE FILLING:
2 tablespoons extra virgin olive oil or Irish rapeseed oil
50 g plain flour

sea salt
freshly ground black pepper
1 kg skirt steak, in chunks
400 g beef kidneys, cored and cut into chunks
150 ml red wine
1 onion, sliced
1 tablespoon tomato ketchup
1 teaspoon English mustard
1 bay leaf
750 ml beef stock
350 g field mushrooms, thickly sliced
one section of marrow bone about 6 cm long
a little milk, for glazing

First make the pastry. In a bowl, mix the flour, baking powder, thyme, salt and pepper. Gently mix in the grated bone marrow and butter, and then add the beaten egg yolks and enough ice-cold milk to bind. Wrap in clingfilm and rest in the fridge for at least an hour.

Heat the oil in a large heavy frying pan until fairly hot but not smoking. Season the flour with fine sea salt and freshly ground black pepper. Toss the chunks of steak and kidney in the seasoned flour, shake off the excess and fry in batches until browned on all sides, adding more oil if needed. Transfer the meat to a large saucepan.

Deglaze the frying pan with the wine, and add the liquid to the meat. Heat a little more oil in the frying pan and cook the onion for a few minutes until softened. Add the onion to the meat, along with the ketchup, mustard, bay leaf and enough stock to just cover the meat. Simmer very gently for about an hour and a half until the meat is just tender. If it is very liquid, remove the meat with a slotted spoon and reduce the sauce over a high heat until thickened. Check the seasoning and leave to cool. You can make the filling up to this point a couple of days ahead.

Preheat the oven to 180° C/fan 160° C/gas mark 5. Fry the mushrooms in a little oil for a couple of minutes and add to the filling.

Fill a pie dish with the meat mixture and place the marrowbone in the centre of the pie like a funnel. Roll out the pastry about 1 cm thick, cut a hole for the marrowbone to poke through, and cover the pie, allowing the excess to hang over the edge. Glaze with milk and bake for 30–40 minutes, or until the pastry is well browned.

Serve with buttered greens and mashed potatoes.

Beef and Crozier Blue Pie with a Suet Crust

April Bloomfield is the British chef behind the Spotted Pig in New York. We took inspiration from a recipe in her book, *A Girl and Her Pig*, to create this luxurious pie that celebrates not only quality beef, but also one of our wonderful Tipperary cheeses, which is produced by the Grubb family, who also make Cashel Blue. You could substitute any similar blue cheese; Bellingham Blue from Co. Louth is another that we like a lot. This is a recipe to be made over a weekend, as it's a two-step process, but by goodness is it worth it. And don't worry if you've never made suet pastry before; it's very forgiving.

You will need a non-stick springform pan, 20 cm in diameter and 8 cm deep.

Serves 6

FOR THE FILLING:
1 kg shin beef, cut into chunks about
  2.5 x 5 cm
1 tablespoon sea salt
freshly ground black pepper
40 g plain flour
100 ml extra virgin olive oil or Irish
  rapeseed oil
2 heads garlic, cloves separated and peeled
2 medium onions, halved lengthwise and
  sliced thickly
2 tablespoons thyme leaves, chopped
1½ tablespoons black peppercorns, coarsely
  crushed
675 ml dry red wine
675 ml chicken stock, preferably homemade

FOR THE SUET PASTRY:
450 g plain flour, plus extra for dusting
1 tablespoon baking powder
2 teaspoons sea salt
150 g freshly ground suet, chilled
about 50 ml ice-cold water

TO FINISH:
butter, at room temperature, for greasing
  the tin
150 g Crozier Blue cheese
1 egg yolk
1 tablespoon whole milk

Put the meat in a big bowl and season it with the salt and pepper. Add the flour and toss, ensuring all pieces are evenly coated.

Put a wide, heavy, ovenproof casserole dish over a high heat and pour in half the oil. When it begins to smoke, brown the meat on all sides in batches, adding more oil as necessary. Transfer the meat to a plate.

Add the garlic, onions, thyme and peppercorns to the pot, and cook, without stirring, for about 3 minutes. Return the meat to the pot, stir well and cook for ten minutes, stirring now and again. Pour in the red wine, stir and bring to a simmer. Turn the heat down to maintain a gentle simmer and cook until the liquid looks a little viscous, about 15 minutes.

Add the stock, return to a simmer, cover the pot and cook at a gentle simmer until the meat is tender, about two hours. Allow the filling to cool in the pot, cover with a lid, and chill overnight in the fridge.

To make the pastry, mix together the flour, baking powder and salt in a medium bowl, then mix in the suet. Add 50 ml water, stirring the mixture with a fork and gradually adding more water if you need it, until you have a slightly sticky dough with the fat well distributed rather than in large chunks. Cover with clingfilm and chill for at least 2 hours and up to 24 hours.

The next day, remove the meat from the pot and put it in a large bowl. There will be about a litre of solidified liquid remaining in the pot. Put the pot over a medium-high heat, bring the liquid to the boil, and cook, stirring frequently to make sure the onion doesn't stick to the bottom, until it has reduced by half, about 45 minutes.

Meanwhile, break the chunks of meat into smaller pieces. Allow the reduced liquid to cool completely and pour it over the meat. Give it a gentle stir.

Grease the tin with the butter. Make a rough ball with ¾ of the dough, keeping the rest in the fridge. Dust the work surface with flour and roll out the dough ball into a 35 cm disc. Place it in the tin, gently pressing it against the bottom and up the sides so it fits securely. Chill in the fridge for at least 15 minutes.

Preheat the oven to 180° C/fan 160° C/gas mark 4. Spoon half the beef filling into the pie shell. Crumble half the cheese into large chunks and scatter over the filling. Spoon in the rest of the filling and scatter with the remaining cheese.

Dust the work surface with flour again. Form the remaining dough into a rough ball and roll it into a circle about 25 cm across. Cut out a circle about 2.5 cm across from the centre of the round and set the small disc aside.

Whisk together the egg yolk and milk in a small bowl. Use a pastry brush to brush the rim of the pie with some of the egg mixture. Lay the 25 cm round on top of the pie and press it lightly against the rim of the bottom crust until it adheres. Trim off any overhang with a knife, reserve it, and crimp the edges.

Form the reserved dough scraps into a ball. Lightly flour the surface again and roll out the dough into a disc about 0.5 cm thick. Cut out a 5 cm circle from the dough, then cut a 2 cm hole in the centre of that, to make an O-shaped piece of dough. Brush the top of the pie with the egg mixture and place the O of dough on top so that the holes line up. Chill for about 15 minutes.

Brush the top of the pie again with the remaining egg mixture and bake, rotating the tin occasionally, until the crust is crisp and golden brown all over, about 1½ hours.

Put the tin on a rack and use a knife to make sure the sides of the crust have separated from the tin. Allow it to rest for about 25 minutes. Carefully loosen the spring and remove the pie. Cut into wedges and serve with a green salad.

Braised Beef Shin and Eight Degrees Ale Pie

Eight Degrees Brewing in Mitchelstown, Co. Cork was set up by an Aussie (Cam) and a Kiwi (Scott) and produces some of Ireland's best craft beers. Caroline Hennessy, who is married to Scott, happens to be a food writer, blogger and a great cook to boot. She kindly gave us this recipe. Over to Caroline:

Serves 4–6

olive oil
1 kg shin of beef, bone removed, trimmed
    and cut into 5 cm pieces
350 g carrots, peeled and cut into thirds
1 large onion, peeled and sliced
2 tablespoons flour
250 ml beef stock
1 x 330 ml bottle Eight Degrees Brewing
    Sunburnt Irish Red Ale
2 teaspoons tomato purée
1 teaspoon Worcestershire sauce
2 bay leaves
3 sprigs of thyme
sea salt
freshly ground black pepper

FOR THE PIE CRUST:
275 g plain flour
3 teaspoons baking powder
pinch salt
50 g butter
250 g milk
a little beaten egg to glaze

Preheat the oven to 170° C/fan 150° C/gas mark 3.
    Heat a little olive oil in a heavy-bottomed casserole over a medium heat. Brown the meat in batches, adding more oil as necessary, then transfer to a bowl. Tip the carrots and onion into the pan and cook until the onion is soft and starting to brown.
    Sprinkle over the flour, cook for a few minutes, then use the beef stock to deglaze the pan, scraping the base of the pan to make sure nothing sticks. Add the beef and ale, tomato purée, Worcestershire sauce, bay leaves and thyme and season well.
    Bring to the boil, cover and place in the preheated oven for at least two hours, or until the meat is tender enough to cut with a spoon. Leave to cool, overnight if possible.
    Meanwhile, make the pie crust by sifting the flour, baking powder and salt into a bowl. Rub in the butter and, using a knife, mix in the milk to make a soft dough. If possible, wrap and refrigerate for 30 minutes before using.
    Preheat the oven to 180° C/fan 160° C/gas mark 4. Dust the worktop with flour and gently roll out the pastry until it is approximately 3 cm thick and large enough to cover your casserole dish.
    Place on top of the pie and cut a hole in the middle to allow steam to escape. Glaze with beaten egg and bake for 35–40 minutes until the pastry is golden brown and the gravy is bubbling.
    Serve with buttered cabbage and some chilled Eight Degrees Brewing Sunburnt Irish Red Ale.

THE SWEETNESS OF SUNBURNT IRISH RED ALE GIVES GREAT FLAVOUR TO THE GRAVY AND CONTRIBUTES A WELCOME BITTERNESS THAT CUTS THROUGH THE RICH MEATY SAUCE.

THIS IS MY GO-TO MAKE-AHEAD MEAL. I NORMALLY COOK THE BEEF A DAY AHEAD OF TIME AND LET IT SIT OVERNIGHT SO THAT THE FLAVOURS CAN BLEND TOGETHER AND THE MEAT IS MELTINGLY TENDER. THE FOLLOWING DAY, IT'S JUST A MATTER OF TOPPING IT WITH THIS SUBSTANTIAL PIE CRUST, WHICH BAKES CRISP ON TOP AND REMAINS SOFT AND SCONE-LIKE UNDERNEATH.

CAROLINE HENNESSY

Rick Stein's Beef, Guinness and Oyster Pie

'In 2002 I was honoured to be named as one of Rick Stein's Food Heroes; it was one of the proudest moments of my career to date. Rick has always encouraged us to think carefully about the food we eat, to seek out the best quality ingredients and to cook them simply. The whole idea of the *Food Heroes* television series was to champion people who were making a difference by offering great-quality local food to their customers. The series saw Rick travel all over Britain and Ireland, searching out the best produce, from beer to bread and from beef to cheese. It was a great accolade to be awarded, and a wonderful endorsement for our family business. The recognition was a great source of pride for the entire community we serve in Tipperary'. – Pat

Serves 6–8

900 g beef stew meat
30 g plain flour
5 tablespoons sunflower oil
30 g unsalted butter
225 g button mushrooms, trimmed
2 onions, thinly sliced
½ teaspoon sugar
300 ml Guinness

300 ml beef stock
3 sprigs fresh thyme
2 bay leaves
2 tablespoons Worcestershire sauce
salt and freshly ground black pepper
12 Pacific oysters
450 g puff pastry
1 small egg, beaten, for brushing

Season the pieces of steak with salt and pepper, then toss with the flour and shake off but reserve the excess. Heat 3 tablespoons of the oil in a flameproof casserole or large saucepan and brown the meat in 2 batches until well coloured on all sides. Transfer to a plate.

Add another tablespoon of the oil, half the butter and the mushrooms to the pan and fry briefly. Set aside with the beef.

Add the rest of the oil and butter, the onions and sugar to the pan and fry over a medium-high heat for 20 minutes, until the onions are nicely browned. Stir in the reserved flour, then gradually add the Guinness and stock and bring to the boil, stirring.

Return the beef and mushrooms to the pan with the thyme, bay leaves, Worcestershire sauce, ¾ teaspoon of salt and some pepper, then cover and simmer for 1½ hours, until the meat is just tender.

Lift the meat, mushrooms and onions out of the liquid with a slotted spoon and put into a deep 1.2 litre pie dish. Bring the liquid to the boil and boil rapidly until reduced to 500 ml. Remove and discard the bay leaves and thyme twigs, adjust the seasoning if necessary and pour into the pie dish. Stir everything together well and leave to cool completely.

Preheat the oven to 200° C/fan 180° C/gas mark 6.

To open the oysters, wrap one hand in a tea towel and hold an oyster in it with the flat shell uppermost. Push the point of an oyster knife into the hinge, located at the narrowest point, and wiggle the knife back and forth until the hinge breaks and you can slide the knife between the shells. Twist the point of the knife upwards to lever up the top shell, cut through the ligament and lift off the top shell. Release the oyster from the bottom shell and remove it, picking out any little bits of shell. Add the oysters to the pie dish and push them well down into the sauce. Push a pie funnel into the centre of the mixture.

Roll out the pastry on a lightly floured surface until it is 2.5 cm larger than the top of the pie dish. Cut off a thin strip from around the edge, brush it with a little beaten egg and press it on to the rim of the dish. Brush it with more egg, cut a small cross into the centre of the larger piece of pastry and lay it over the dish so that the funnel pokes through the cross. Press the edges together well to seal. Trim away the excess overhanging pastry and crimp the edges between your fingers to give it an attractive finish. Chill for 20 minutes to relax the pastry.

Brush the top of the pie with beaten egg and bake for 30 to 35 minutes, until the pastry is crisp and golden and the filling is bubbling hot.

Individual Potato-Topped Steak and Chorizo Pies

These cute little pies are lovely for supper with a simple green salad on the side. The chorizo makes for added interest and flavour. Children love these pies.

Serves 6

50 g butter
freshly ground black pepper
fine sea salt
500 g onions, minced
500 g minced beef
200 g cooking chorizo, finely chopped

50 g flour
200 ml beef stock
2 tablespoons Worcestershire sauce
3 large potatoes, peeled and thinly sliced
50 g butter, melted

Melt the butter in a large frying pan and season with lots of pepper and some salt. Add the onions and cook until soft but not brown. Add the mince and chorizo and cook for another five minutes. Sprinkle with the flour and cook for a couple of minutes more, then add the stock and Worcestershire sauce, bring to the boil, and simmer for 10 minutes until cooked through.

Preheat the oven to 240° C/fan 220° C/gas mark 9.

Grease 6 individual pie dishes. Spoon the filling into the dishes and top with the sliced potatoes. Brush the potato with lots of melted butter, then put the pies into the oven and bake for about 35 minutes until nicely browned.

Cottage Pie with Porcini Mushrooms

If you are not a mushroom fan, you can leave out the porcini or replace them with some chopped pancetta or bacon.

Serves 6

20 g dried porcini
2 tablespoons extra virgin olive oil or Irish rapeseed oil
1 kg minced beef
1 onion, chopped
2 garlic cloves, crushed
3 tablespoons plain flour
1 × 400 g tin chopped tomatoes
150 ml red wine

salt and freshly ground black pepper
2 tablespoons fresh thyme leaves, chopped
2 tablespoons Worcestershire sauce
1 kg floury potatoes, peeled
5 tablespoons milk
a large knob of butter
75 g Hegarty's cheddar

Preheat the oven to 160° C/fan 140° C/gas mark 3.

Soak the porcini in a bowl with 400 ml boiling water for 30 minutes, then drain, reserving the liquid, and chop the porcini. Heat the oil in a casserole dish, add the mince and fry in batches until well browned. Add the onion and garlic and fry for a few minutes. Sprinkle over the flour, stir for a minute, then add the chopped tomatoes, wine, mushrooms and reserved mushroom liquid. Stir and season with salt and pepper. Bring to the boil, cover and cook in the oven for 45 minutes to 1 hour, or until the mince is tender.

Remove from the oven and stir in the thyme and Worcestershire sauce. Taste to check the seasoning. Transfer the mince into a shallow pie dish and spread out evenly. Set aside to cool while you make the topping.

Increase the oven temperature to 200° C/fan 180° C/gas mark 6.

Boil the potatoes in salted water until tender. Drain and return to the pan. Add the milk, butter, salt and pepper and mash until smooth. Spread the potatoes over the mince and make ridges on the top with the tines of a fork. Sprinkle with the cheese then place in the oven for 35–40 minutes, until bubbling and golden on top.

Chapter 9
The Other Bits

For decades it seemed as if no once wanted to eat anything other than steak, but we have noticed a real resurgence of interest in what we call 'the other bits', which can make for such interesting eating. Here are a few suggestions that should get you started.

Liver and Onions with a Mushroom Sauce

This is less a recipe than a dish that Pat cooks for his family as a quick supper when he is on dinner duty. His children love liver prepared in this simple way, with a big dollop of mashed potato served alongside.

Serves 4

800 g beef liver
500 ml whole milk
2 tablespoons extra virgin olive or Irish
　rapeseed oil
600 g onions, sliced
sea salt

freshly ground black pepper
70 g butter
600 g mushrooms, sliced
150 ml stock or wine

Cut the liver in strips as if preparing it for a stir fry and soak it in the milk for a couple of hours, covered, in the fridge.

Heat the oil in a large frying pan and add the onions. Cook slowly, for about 30 minutes, over a low to medium heat until soft and caramelised. Set aside and keep warm.

Discard the milk and pat the strips of liver dry with kitchen paper. Season with sea salt and freshly ground black pepper. Heat half the butter in another frying pan and cook the strips of liver over a high heat for only a few minutes, until the strips are starting to catch on the outside but are still pink in the middle. Set to one side, covered with foil, and add the rest of the butter and the mushrooms to the pan.

Cook over a high heat until the mushrooms are nicely browned, and then add the stock or wine to the pan and let it bubble up. Stir to make sure you get all the bits of flavour from the pan into the sauce, season with sea salt and plenty of black pepper.

Serve the liver topped with the mushroom sauce and with the onions on the side.

Tongue and Roast Beetroot Salad with a Balsamic Dressing

Lots of people these days seem to be nostalgic for the ox tongue of their childhood, but few attempt to cook it. A whole ox tongue does look rather terrifying, admittedly, but we think it's worth the effort. Brining the tongue before you cook it gives the meat great flavour, but does turn it into almost a week-long project. You have been warned.

Serves 6

1 ox tongue

FOR THE BRINE:
100 g sea salt
2 tablespoons black peppercorns
1 tablespoon whole cloves
3 fresh bay leaves
¾ teaspoon curing salt (this is for colour
    rather than flavour and can be omitted)

TO COOK THE TONGUE:
1 carrot, chopped
1 onion, chopped
1 stick celery, chopped
handful of parsley stalks
6 black peppercorns
flaky sea salt
3 eggs
100 g plain flour
250 g panko breadcrumbs
1 litre vegetable oil

FOR THE SALAD:
8 medium beetroots roasted (see page 113)
300 g mixed leaves
extra virgin olive oil
aged balsamic vinegar

In a large saucepan, combine the salt, peppercorns, cloves, and bay leaves in a litre of water. Bring to the boil and stir until the salt has dissolved. Remove from the heat and add 2 litres of cold water. Leave to cool.

Place the tongue in a large bowl and cover with the brine. Place in the fridge, covered, for five days, turning once.

Remove the tongue from the brine, rinse well, put in a large pot and cover with water. Bring to the boil and discard the water. Cover with fresh water and bring to the boil again, and add the carrot, onion, celery and parsley stalks, peppercorns and a large pinch of flaky sea salt. Simmer gently until tender but not falling apart, about 4 to 5 hours.

Remove the tongue from the cooking liquid but retain the liquid. When the tongue is cool enough to handle, strip it of its skin and any unsavoury-looking bits. Return the tongue to the cooking liquid to cool. When it has reached room temperature, remove from the liquid and place it in a bowl in the fridge, with a weight on top of it to press it down, for 24 hours.

Prepare the roasted beetroots.

Whisk the eggs and place in a shallow bowl. Prepare separate bowls for the flour and breadcrumbs. Slice the tongue into slices about ½ cm thick. Heat the vegetable oil to 190° C in a deep fat fryer.

Dip the slices of tongue first into the flour, then the egg, then the breadcrumbs. Fry in the hot oil until golden brown and hot through. Drain on kitchen paper.

Dress the leaves and roasted beetroots with olive oil and a little flaky sea salt and divide between six plates. Place the slices of fried tongue on each plate and top with a drizzle of aged balsamic vinegar.

Roast Bone Marrow with Desmond Cheese

This is a rich and very tasty starter, probably best followed by a light main course. Or a nice lie-down.

Serves 4

**4 sections of marrow bones, abut 10 cm long,
  split lengthways
sea salt
freshly ground black pepper
smoked sea salt
100 g Desmond cheese, finely grated**

Preheat the oven to 200° C/fan 180° C/gas mark 6.
    Lightly season the exposed sides of the marrow bones and roast in the oven for 6–8 minutes until the marrow is soft. Sprinkle the surface with the cheese and a little smoked sea salt and place under the grill until nicely browned. Serve with toasted sourdough bread.

IF I HAD THOUGHT THE BEEF MARROW MIGHT BE A HELL OF A LOT OF WORK FOR NOT MUCH DIFFERENCE, I NEEDN'T HAVE WORRIED. THE TASTE OF THE MARROW IS RICH, MEATY, INTENSE IN A NEARLY-TOO-MUCH WAY. IN MY INCREASINGLY DEPRAVED STATE, I COULD THINK OF NOTHING AT FIRST BUT THAT IT TASTED LIKE REALLY GOOD SEX. BUT THERE WAS SOMETHING MORE THAN THAT, EVEN. WHAT IT REALLY TASTES LIKE IS LIFE, WELL LIVED. OF COURSE THE COW I GOT MARROW FROM HAD A FAIRLY CRAPPY LIFE – LOTS OF CROWDS AND OVERMEDICATION AND BLAND FOOD THAT MIGHT OR MIGHT NOT HAVE BEEN A RELATIVE. BUT DEEP IN HIS OR HER BONES, THERE WAS A CAPACITY FOR FERAL JOY. I COULD TASTE IT.

JULIE POWELL, *JULIE AND JULIA: MY YEAR OF COOKING DANGEROUSLY*

Fergus Henderson's Signature Bone Marrow and Parsley Salad

Fergus Henderson is the man behind London's celebrated St John restaurant and is credited with the revival in nose to tail eating that began in earnest a couple of decades ago. Henderson's version of this salad, which is never off the menu at St John, is made with veal marrow bones, but the dish works just as well with beef.

At the West Waterford Food Festival in 2013, the dish was cooked at the FergusStock dinner by Paul Flynn of The Tannery in Dungarvan to honour Fergus Henderson. Pat supplied the bones, as well as ox hearts that were served with horseradish and beetroot. Also on the menu was a pot-roast half pig's head, supplied by TJ Crowe. It all tasted wonderful.

Serves 4

12 x 7–8 cm pieces of marrow bone
leaves from a large bunch of flat-leaf parsley
2 shallots, peeled and very thinly sliced
1 modest handful of capers, extra fine if
   possible
a good supply of toast

FOR THE DRESSING:
juice of 1 lemon
extra virgin olive oil
a pinch of sea salt and black pepper

Preheat the oven to hot, about 230° C/210° C/gas mark 8.

Put the bone marrow in an ovenproof frying pan and place in the oven. The roasting process should take about 20 minutes, depending on the thickness of the bone. You are looking for the marrow to be loose and giving, not melted away, which it will do if left too long.

Meanwhile, lightly chop the parsley, mix it with the shallots and capers, and dress the salad at the last moment.

To eat, scrape the marrow from the bone on to the toast, season with coarse sea salt and add a pinch of parsley salad on top.

Bone Marrow Mash

3 large marrow bones, split
4 medium potatoes, peeled
1 small onion, thinly sliced
1 leek, white part only, thinly sliced

1 tablespoon extra virgin olive or Irish
  rapeseed oil
a knob of butter
sea salt and freshly ground black pepper

Preheat the oven to 190° C/fan 170° C/gas mark 5.

Roast the marrow bones for about 15 minutes until they are nicely browned but the marrow is still holding together. Cut the potatoes into evenly sized chunks and boil in salted water until tender. Drain and set to one side. In a frying pan over medium heat, sauté the onion and leek in the oil until soft and starting to brown.

In a large bowl, mash the potatoes with the butter. Add the marrow from the bones and continue to mash until there are no lumps. Add the leek and onions and combine. Season with sea salt and freshly ground black pepper to taste.

Beef Heart Skewers with Chimichurri

The heart is muscle rather than organ meat. It takes a little effort to trim all the sinew away, but we think it's worth the trouble.

Serves 6

1 beef heart, trimmed and cut into slices or
  chunks
sea salt
freshly ground black pepper
1 large shallot, roughly chopped

2 tablespoons extra virgin olive or Irish
  rapeseed oil
6 handfuls rocket
1 quantity chimichurri sauce (see page 45)

Season the beef with sea salt and freshly ground black pepper. Add the shallot and the oil, mix together and refrigerate for an hour, covered with clingfilm.

Thread the meat on to skewers and grill for about 2 to 3 minutes per side. You can cook the skewers either on a griddle pan or outside on the barbecue. If you're using a charcoal barbecue, wait until the coals have completely ashed over before cooking the skewers.

Serve with rocket and chimichurri.

Oxtail Soup with Pearl Barley

Perhaps because it smacked of post-war austerity, oxtail soup fell out of favour for many years, but it is almost modish these days. There's no denying that it's a slow, though not labour-intensive, business, and you need to start the day before you want to eat it, but if you are pottering around the kitchen for the day anyway, we can think of worse uses for that small ring at the back of the cooker.

Serves 6

70 g butter
1.5 kg oxtail, cut into pieces
2 celery stalks, sliced
1 onion, stuck with 3 cloves
2 carrots, sliced
3 small white turnips, peeled, quartered and
    sliced
1 leek, roughly chopped
1 bouquet garni (made up of a bay leaf, a
    couple of sprigs of thyme and three or four
    parsley stalks, tied together with kitchen
    string)

10 black peppercorns
300 ml red wine
salt and freshly ground black pepper
150 g pearl barley
60–80 ml sherry
3 tablespoons finely chopped parsley

Heat the butter in a large heavy-bottomed pan over medium heat and brown the oxtail pieces on all sides, in batches. Remove from the pan and set aside. Add the vegetables to the pan and cook for about five minutes, or until starting to soften.

Return the meat to the pan with the bouquet garni, peppercorns, wine and 2 litres of water. Season, bring to a boil and simmer very slowly, covered, until the meat is very tender and falling off the bones. This will take anything up to four hours.

Strain the broth into a bowl, cool and refrigerate. Discard the vegetables, peppercorns and herbs. Pull the meat from the bones, discarding any skin and fat. Place in a bowl, season, allow to cool and refrigerate.

Next day, remove the solid layer of fat that will have formed on the top of the stock, pour the stock into a pan and bring to a gentle simmer. Add the pearl barley. When the grains are almost tender, add the meat and cook for another five minutes. Adjust the seasoning to taste, add the sherry and simmer very gently for five minutes. Serve in warmed bowls, scattered with chopped parsley.

Savoury Mince on Beef Dripping Fried Bread

Do you remember when there used to be a little jar of fat lurking at the back of everyone's fridge? The habit of accumulating the fat left in the pan after roasting a joint of beef has all but disappeared, but we think it's deserving of a revival. If you pour the fatty residue into a glass Kilner jar, you'll see that there's a top layer of white fat and a lower layer of dark and delicious meat juices. The white fat is good for cooking, the meaty juices delicious on toast. In this recipe we fry bread in the white fat and serve it with a piquant, anchovy-flavoured mince that takes us way back.

Serves 4

1 tablespoon extra virgin olive or Irish
  rapeseed oil
1 small onion, finely chopped
400 g minced beef
4 anchovies, finely chopped
2 tablespoons plain flour
150 ml beef stock

2 tablespoons Worcestershire sauce
flaky sea salt
freshly ground black pepper

4 slices sourdough bread
4 tablespoons beef dripping (white part)

Heat the oil in a frying pan and sauté the onion until soft and starting to brown. Add the minced beef and the anchovies and stir until all trace of pinkness has disappeared from the meat.

Sprinkle with the flour and add the stock. Simmer over a low heat for about 20 minutes until it has reached a thick, sauce-like consistency. Add the Worcestershire sauce and season to taste.

Heat the dripping in a frying pan and fry the bread until golden. Serve with the mince.

Dripping Toast

Dripping toast hardly needs a recipe – just toast a slice of good white bread (sourdough is particularly tasty) and spread with the jelly-like meat juices and sediment that accumulate at the bottom of a jar of dripping. Sprinkle with flaky sea salt.

Beef Stock

There's great satisfaction to be had from a freezer full of homemade stock. Roasting the bones followed by long, slow simmering to extract every last smidgeon of flavour is one of those activities best suited to a day when there is nothing else planned bar pottering around the kitchen, feeling thrifty and ever so slightly smug. Because it's a time-consuming process, it's worth doing when you have a significant quantity of bones to make the effort worthwhile.

raw beef bones, as many as your butcher will give you or your stockpot will accommodate
a few carrots, onions and sticks of celery – 1 each per kilo of bones
black peppercorns – 6 per kilo of bones
bay leaves – 1 per kilo of bones

Pre-heat the oven to 220° C/fan 200° C/gas mark 8. Roast the bones in a large sturdy roasting tray until lightly browned. Pour off the fat and reserve for dripping.

Place the bones in a large stockpot with the vegetables, peppercorns and bay leaves and bring to the boil, then immediately reduce the heat to the merest simmer. Simmer for 4–5 hours.

Remove the bones, vegetables, peppercorns and bay leaves. Strain the liquid through a fine sieve and leave to cool. Refrigerate overnight and the fat will rise to the top. Skim off the hard fat and place the now jelly-like stock into 1 litre freezer bags. Label the bags with the date and freeze.

> # STOCK IS EVERYTHING IN COOKING, WITHOUT IT NOTHING CAN BE DONE.
>
> ## AUGUSTE ESCOFFIER

Conversion Charts

Metric	Imperial	Metric	Imperial
5 g	⅛ oz	325 g	11½ oz
10 g	¼ oz	350 g	12 oz
15 g	½ oz	375 g	13 oz
20 g	¾ oz	400 g	14 oz
25 g	1 oz	425 g	15 oz
35 g	1¼ oz	450 g	1 lb
40 g	1½ oz	500 g	1 lb 2 oz
50 g	1¾ oz	550 g	1 lb 4 oz
55 g	2 oz	600 g	1 lb 5 oz
60 g	2¼ oz	650 g	1 lb 7 oz
70 g	2½ oz	700 g	1 lb 9 oz
75 g	2¾ oz	750 g	1 lb 10 oz
85 g	3 oz	800 g	1 lb 12 oz
90 g	3¼ oz	850 g	1 lb 14 oz
100 g	3½ oz	900 g	2 lb
115 g	4 oz	950 g	2 lb 2 oz
125 g	4½ oz	1 kg	2 lb 4 oz
140 g	5 oz	1.25 kg	2 lb 12 oz
150 g	5½ oz	1.3 kg	3 lb
175 g	6 oz	1.5 kg	3 lb 5 oz
200 g	7 oz	1.6 kg	3 lb 8 oz
225 g	8 oz	1.8 kg	4 lb
250 g	9 oz	2 kg	4 lb 8 oz
275 g	9¾ oz	2.25 kg	5 lb
280 g	10 oz	2.5 kg	5 lb 8 oz
300 g	10½ oz	2.7 kg	6 lb
315 g	11 oz	3 kg	6 lb 8 oz

Oven Temperatures

Celcius	Fahrenheit	Gas
110°C	225°F	¼
120°C	250°F	½
140°C	275°F	1
150°C	300°F	2
160°C	325°F	3
170°C	325°F	3
180°C	350°F	4
190°C	375°F	5
200°C	400°F	6
220°C	425°F	7
230°C	450°F	8

Spoons

Metric	Imperial
1.25 ml	¼ tsp
2.5 ml	½ tsp
5 ml	1 tsp
10 ml	2 tsp
15 ml	3 tsp/1 tbsp
30 ml	2 tbsp
45 ml	3 tbsp
60 ml	4 tbsp
75 ml	5 tbsp
90 ml	6 tbsp

US Cups

Cups	Metric
¼ cup	60 ml
⅓ cup	70 ml
½ cup	125 ml
⅔ cup	150 ml
¾ cup	175 ml
1 cup	250 ml
1½ cups	375 ml
2 cups	500 ml
3 cups	750 ml
4 cups	1 litre

Volume

Metric	Imperial	Metric	Imperial	Metric	Imperial
25 ml	1 fl oz	300 ml	10 fl oz	1 litre	1¼ pints
50 ml	2 fl oz	350 ml	12 fl oz	1.2 litres	2 pints
75 ml	2½ fl oz	400 ml	14 fl oz	1.3 litres	2¼ pints
100 ml	3½ fl oz	425 ml	15 fl oz	1.4 litres	2½ pints
125 ml	4 fl oz	450 ml	16 fl oz	1.5 litres	2¾ pints
150 ml	5 fl oz	500 ml	18 fl oz	1.7 litres	3 pints
175 ml	6 fl oz	568 ml	20 fl oz	2 litres	3½ pints
200 ml	7 fl oz	600 ml	1 pint	2.5 litres	4½ pints
225 ml	8 fl oz	700 ml	1¼ pints	2.8 litres	5 pints
250 ml	9 fl oz	850 ml	1½ pints	3 litres	5¼ pints

Appendix:
Tipperary Food Producers

Sarah Baker
Cloughjordan House
Cloughjordan
0505 42492
087 969 0824
sarahbakercs@gmail.com
Cookery school

Mags Bergin
Mags' Home Baking
Shesheraghkeale
Limerick Road
Nenagh
067 33958
086 841 9331
mags@magshomebaking.ie
Cakes and breads

John Brett
Moneyvale Foods
Cahir
052 744 1600
info@oakparkfoods.ie
Bacon

Kate and Michael Cantwell
Boulabán Farm Ice Cream
Roscrea
0505 43111
086 262 6348
kmcantwell@eircom.net
Ice creams and sorbets

John Commins
Blackcastle
Two Mile Borris
Thurles
087 913 5349
info@irishpiemontesebeef.ie
Beef

Valerie Cotter
Terryglass Treats
Cornalack
Terryglass
terryglasstreats@eircom.net
Chocolates

TJ Crowe
Crowe Farm Meats
Gortussa
Dundrum
062 71137
087 824 7394
info@crowefarm.ie
tjcrowe@crowefarm.ie
Pork, bacon, traditional sausages

Malachy Dorris
Lough Derg Chocolates
Newtown
Nenagh
087 968 3534
malachydorris@yahoo.com
Chocolates

Egan Family
Inch House
Thurles
0504 51348
mairin@inchhouse.ie
Black and white pudding and chutneys

Sarah Furno
J&L Grubb Ltd
Beechmount
Fethard
052 613 1151
086 172 1443
info@cashelblue.com
Cashel Blue and Crozier Blue cheese

Bernard Geraghty
The Green Bowl Company
Derrygrath Lower
Cahir
086 034 2331
thegreenbowlcompany@gmail.com
Salads

Gary Gubbins
Red Nose Wine
Clonmel Business Park
Clonmel
052 618 2939
086 332 6486
info@rednosewine.com
Artisan wine importer

Nuala Hickey
Hickeys Bakery
West Gate
Clonmel
052 612 1587
087 274 8637
hickey.nuala@gmail.com
Old-fashioned bread, grinder bread, barm brack

Ann Keating
Baylough Cheese
Clogheen
052 746 5275
Farmhouse cheese

Breda and Jim Maher
Cooleeney Farmhouse
Moyne, Thurles
0504 45112/086 241 6250
cooleeney@eircom.net
Farmhouse cheese

Cate McCarthy
The Cookie Jar
Graigue
Poulmucka
Clonmel
086 388 1280
thecookiejar@eircom.net
Cookies

Veronica Molloy
Crossogue Preserves
Crossogue House
Ballycahill
0504 54416
info@crossoguepreserves.com
Jams, jellies, marmalades, chutneys

Eddie O'Donnell
O'Donnells Crisps
Seskin Farm
Kilsheelan
052 613 9016
087 255 8142
info@odonnellscrisps.com
Crisps

Una O'Dwyer
Una O'Dwyer Fine Foods
Deansgrove
Cashel
062 65889
una@unaodwyerfinefoods.ie
*Traditional sausages, black and white
puddings*

Florrie Purcell
The Scullery
Kilkeary
Norwood
Nenagh
086 174 4402
florrie@thescullery.ie
Glazes and relishes

Barbara Russell
Barbara Russell Catering
Kilmanahan
Clonmel
052 613 6943
086 811 0749
russellcatering@iol.ie
www.barbararussellcatering.ie
Caterer

Michael Seymour
Sheepwalk
Finnoe Road
Borrisokane
086 400 0680
seymourorganic@gmail.com
Organic lamb and beef

Con and Catherine Traas
The Apple Farm
Moorstown
Cahir
052 744 1459
con@theapplefarm.com
Apple juice, seasonal fruits, apple jelly

Ann Marie Walsh
Tipperary Kitchen
Holycross
Thurles
086 824 6310
annmarie@thetipperarykitchen.ie
Breads, sauces, confectionery

Lavinia and Donal Walsh
Munster Mushrooms
Silverford
Fethard
052 6131074
lavinia@munstermushrooms.ie
Mushrooms

Pat Whelan
James Whelan Butchers
Oakville Shopping Centre
Clonmel
052 618 2477
pat@jameswhelanbutchers.com
Beef and lamb

Index